DR RADCLIFFE'S LIBRARY

ANNO   *A Perspective View of the outside*   1747
              of the RADCLIFFE LIBRARY.

Jacob Gibbs Architect   *P. Fourdrinier Sculp.*

Stephen Hebron

Dr Radcliffe's Library

*The Story of the
Radcliffe Camera
in Oxford*

Bodleian Library
UNIVERSITY OF OXFORD

First published in 2014 by the Bodleian Library
Broad Street
Oxford OX1 3BG

www.bodleianbookshop.co.uk

ISBN: 978 1 85124 429 4

Cover design by Dot Little at the Bodleian Library
Designed and typeset by Stephen Hebron in 11/13 pt Monotype Baskerville
Printed and bound by TJ International Ltd., Padstow, Cornwall
on 90gsm munken paper

British Library Catalogue in Publishing Data
A CIP record of this publication is available from the British Library

Contents

Illustrations

All images are Bodleian Libraries unless otherwise stated.

Colour plates:

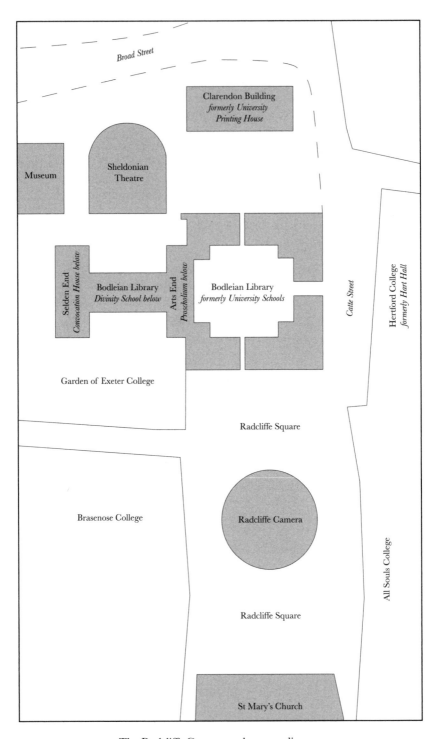

1. The Radcliffe Camera and surrounding area.

⮞ I ⮜
The Legacy

At the end of November 1714, members of Oxford University were told that an important funeral would take place the following week. A printed notice signed by the Vice-Chancellor (the senior officer of the university) provided the details and gave instructions. On Wednesday, 1 December, the body of Dr John Radcliffe, 'our most Munificent Benefactor', would arrive in Oxford. It would be met at the great gate of the University Schools by the Vice-Chancellor, the Proctors (the officers responsible for university discipline) and members of Convocation (the University's legislative body). The assembled academics would then follow the coffin to the Divinity School, where Radcliffe's embalmed body would lay in public view. At midday on Friday the great bell of the University Church of St Mary the Virgin would toll, and all members of Convocation were to proceed to Convocation House. There, instructed the Vice-Chancellor, they were to sit in their places while a Latin oration was delivered over the body, 'which on that Occasion is to be remov'd thither'. The company was then to process, by way of Brasenose, Lincoln, Exeter and Jesus Colleges, to St Mary's for the funeral service. All students, meanwhile, were 'strictly commanded to behave themselves in a manner suitable to so solemn an Occasion.' On no account were they to interrupt the procession, 'tear off the Escutcheons', or make any disturbance in the church.

It was indeed a solemn and impressive event. Radcliffe's fine elm coffin arrived in Oxford on a hearse drawn by six grey horses and decorated with assorted plumes, escutcheons, banners, streamers and shields. On its journey from the doctor's estate, at Carshalton in Surrey, the hearse had been attended by ten pages in mourning; twenty men had ridden before it on white horses, and after it had followed six coaches, each drawn by six horses. Over 300 Masters of Arts paid their respects to Radcliffe's corpse while it lay in the Divinity School, and all were given a gold mourning ring and a pair of mourning gloves. The walls of the Divinity School, a fine fifteenth-century Gothic chamber, were covered with dozens of escutcheons and great hangings of black cloth; the body was encircled by a rail of state covered with velvet, by twelve silver candlesticks, and plumes of black and white feathers. As the funeral procession followed the coffin to the church – Radcliffe's nephews and Executors in their long mourning dress, the bishops in their robes, the academics in their variously coloured gowns and hoods – a bell tolled at every one of the University's colleges and halls. The church was arrayed in numerous hangings and coverings and the area around the grave filled with trophies. Everything was done on the grandest scale: altogether, the Vice-Chancellor's expenses and the bills of the parish, the funeral director, the carpenter, the mason and the goldsmiths came to more than £700.

Who was this munificent benefactor whose death could occasion such elaborate funeral rites, and bring the senior members of the University, on successive winter days, from their studies and common rooms?

John Radcliffe was the most successful doctor of his day. He came from Wakefield in Yorkshire, where he was baptized in 1650 and where his father served as governor of the city's house of correction. He received a good education at the local grammar school, and in 1666, aged fifteen, he entered University College, Oxford.

Radcliffe spent the next eighteen years in Oxford. His progress from young scholar to successful doctor was rapid and relatively smooth. In 1667, thanks to his skill in rhetoric and logical dispute, he was awarded a senior scholarship, and in 1669 he earned his degree as a Bachelor of Arts. There were no vacant fellowships at his own college, so he became a Fellow of Lincoln College, where he studied anatomy, botany and chemistry. In 1672 he became a Master of Arts and began to study for the Bachelor of Medicine, which he duly received in 1675. Now licensed as a physician he immediately set up a medical practice, working first from his college rooms, and then, having resigned his fellowship at Lincoln, from lodgings in town.

Although he would never be at the intellectual forefront of his profession, Radcliffe was highly intelligent and free from the obscurantism that held back many doctors. As a student he put aside the old medical treatises and read the work of progressive physicians like Thomas Sydenham and Thomas Willis, who believed in clinical observation and the scientific investigation of human anatomy. As a young doctor Radcliffe had an engaging personal manner and a flair for diagnosis. He administered moderate and sensible treatments. At a time when smallpox was rife in Oxfordshire he rejected common practice, which confined the patient to a hot, airless room, and applied Sydenham's 'cooling treatment': cold emulsions, and plenty of fresh air. Consequently, his practice thrived: Radcliffe's surviving pocket-books from his Oxford years show that he enjoyed both a steady demand for his services and a healthy income, and when he successfully treated the invalid wife of Sir Thomas Spencer, the well-connected lord of nearby Yarnton, the local nobility soon featured prominently in his list of patients.

In 1682 Radcliffe graduated as a Doctor of Medicine. There was nothing more to keep him in Oxford, and so two years later, aged 32, he moved to London and established a practice at Bow Street, Covent Garden. For the next three decades he worked with great industry and consistent success. 'He had little or no Learning,' the Oxford antiquary Thomas Hearne later wrote, 'but he had a strange Sagacity, and was so wonderfully successful in the Practise of Physick, yet he never had his equal by which he got such a vast sum of Money.' Radcliffe had a happy habit of curing people: 'every patient who was in despair turned his fading eyes on him alone', said Dr James Munro in 1737, 'as one who could remove every cause of sickness and aid the course of events'. A collection of his medical prescriptions, *Pharmacopoeia Radcliffeana*, was published two years after his death, and quickly sold out.

In person, Radcliffe was a colourful character. He liked his food and drink, and relished lively conversation in taverns. His readiness to criticize others, particularly fellow doctors, and the blunt way he had of expressing his strictures, was refreshing but could also be deeply offensive. His robust sense of humour was entertaining but sometimes crude. Gregarious but tactless, witty but vulgar, Radcliffe was a vivid and unpredictable presence in London society. He left almost no record of his private thoughts, concerns or ambitions in the form of letters or diary entries, but thanks to his celebrity we have plenty of anecdotes describing his more outrageous moments and livelier utterances. Some are more credible than others, but all were faithfully recorded by his first biographer, William Pittis, who dashed off an account of the famous physician's life within a year of his death.

Politically Radcliffe was a staunch Tory and a Jacobite; for five years he served as a Member of Parliament for Bramber, a village in Sussex (number of voters, thirty-seven); but he observed a certain caution in politics that enabled him to attend to members of the royal family during the reigns both of James II and of William and Mary. Two years after moving to London he was appointed principal physician to James II's daughter, Princess Anne of Denmark. Following William's accession to the throne he was regularly called to court, and earned the king's favour when he cured two of his most valued attendants. In 1689 he relieved the king of an asthma attack, and in 1695, at William's request, he successfully treated the Earl of Albemarle, one of the king's favourite commanders. But Radcliffe would eventually offend the king. In 1697 he found William suffering from dropsy and told him that provided he mended his ways, particularly his excessive drinking, he could expect to live for another three or four years. Called to the palace again in 1700, Radcliffe saw that William had reverted to his old habits. Asked by the anxious king what he made of his horribly swollen ankles, he reportedly replied: 'Why truly, I would not have your Majesty's two legs for your three kingdoms.' The king never forgave his doctor for this ill-advised witticism.

Radcliffe's relationship with Princess, later Queen, Anne was similarly erratic. In 1688 he refused to visit the princess in Nottingham when she became pregnant with the future Duke of Gloucester, arguing that he could not abandon his London patients. Two years later he was summoned to Windsor, where the infant Duke was having convulsions. He successfully treated him with bark, and in the process earned himself 1,000 guineas. In 1695, however, he gravely offended Princess Anne by failing to respond to an urgent summons to St James's Palace. Apparently the message came to Radcliffe while he was in a tavern, and when a second messenger was despatched he is said to have exclaimed hotly: 'By God! Her Highness's distemper is nothing but the vapours, and she is in as good a state of health as any woman breathing, could she but give in to the belief of it.' When he finally arrived at the palace the following morning he was intercepted by a courtier and turned away.

Sometimes Radcliffe was only called to the royal bedside after other doctors had failed, and on such occasions he was quick to express his contempt for his fellow practitioners. Physicians in the eighteenth century, with their gold-headed canes, were respected members of society, but the effectiveness of their treatments was by no means certain and the public could be sceptical of their proclaimed knowledge. Nor was the profession free from the quackery mocked by Hogarth in his print *The Company of Undertakers* (fig. 2). So doctors did not take it kindly when their skills were impugned by the celebrated Dr Radcliffe. In 1694 he

2. William Hogarth, *The Company of Undertakers*, 1736.

was summoned by the privy council to attend Queen Mary, who had contracted smallpox. He first looked at the treatment she had been having, then promptly said, loudly, that it was bound to kill her, and that there was nothing he could do for her. She died soon afterwards. In 1700 he was called to the Duke of Gloucester, now eleven and gravely ill with suspected smallpox. Having told the two hapless doctors who had been ministering to the patient that by bleeding him they had as good as killed him, he applied blisters. There was some improvement, but the child soon relapsed and died.

Radcliffe never regained Anne's favour, and in the summer of 1714 notoriously refused to attend the dying queen. He later maintained that his presence would only have hastened her end and that the request had not come to him through official channels, but the grieving public were unimpressed. Radcliffe's friend Sir George Beaumont wrote to him shortly after the queen's death: 'today the Mob as well as Quality have expressed so much Resentment against you that if your new House had stood at London or Kensington they would scarce be restrained from pulling it down. They all agree that if any one could have saved the Queen Dr Radcliffe could, and that it's possible if he could have been prevailed with to come she might have lived'.

Radcliffe himself died a few months after this infamous episode, on 1 November 1714, aged 64. He had never married, and in the course of his career had accumulated a sizeable fortune. On his death he owned a large house in Bloomsbury Square, a mansion in Surrey, and estates in Buckinghamshire, Yorkshire and Northamptonshire. A glance at the sale catalogue of the contents of his London home shows that he lived in some style: the best furniture; fine ornaments; plenty of silver plate; a large and impressive wine cellar; paintings by Rubens, Hals, Breugel, Rembrandt, Poussin and Van Dyck.

In the weeks before his death Radcliffe made a final will. Avarice, he told himself, had been his principal sin, and he wished to make up for it. In an uncharacteristically reflective mood he told his sister Millicent: '[I] can plead nothing in excuse, but that the Love of Money, which I have emphatically known to be Root of all Evil, was too predominant over me. Though, I hope, I have made some Amends for that odious Sin of Covetousness, in my last Dispositions of those worldly Goods, which it pleas'd the great Dispenser of Providence to bless me with.' He made generous provision for Millicent and his other sister, Hannah, for his nephews and for his servants. He then made a number of bequests, after the payment of which, he directed, any surplus should be put to whatever charitable uses his Executors thought best. Among these bequests was a gift to St Bartholomew's Hospital in London of £500 a year 'towards mending their Diet' and £100 a year 'for buying Linen'. The main beneficiary, however, was the University of Oxford.

It was thirty years since Radcliffe had lived in Oxford, but according to his biographer, William Pittis, he had decided to leave his fortune to 'the Place of his Education' in 1694, 'as may be seen from his Answer to a Man of Fashion, who, after asking him, *Why did he not marry some young Gentlewoman to get his Heirs by*, had by way of Reply, *That truly he had an old One to take care of, which he intended to be his Executrix*.' He had kept in touch with the University through a number of friends who may individually have convinced him that his Alma Mater was a fitting recipient of his riches, and what is more that it provided an opportunity for him to memorialize his life. The friends were Arthur Charlett, the self-important Master of University College and an incorrigible gossip; Henry Aldrich, the Dean of Christ Church, and George Clarke, a politician and Fellow of All Souls College. Aldrich was one of Radcliffe's closest friends. A scholar, a talented musician and a great collector of books, manuscripts, drawings and prints, he was also an accomplished draughtsman and amateur architect. He designed the allegorical scenes that headed the Oxford Almanack (the University calendar), and generally acted as an arbiter of taste for the University. Radcliffe asked Aldrich to arrange a memorial over his grave and to compose his epitaph, but his friend pre-deceased him, dying under his care in 1710. George Clarke succeeded Aldrich as Oxford's *arbiter elegantiae* and took over the design of the Almanack. He was also an amateur architect, and played a central role in the architectural development of Oxford in the early eighteenth century.

In his will Radcliffe left £600 a year to the University for two ten-year fellowships, eligible to Oxford students who were Masters of Arts 'and entered on the Physic line'. They were to spend half their time 'in parts beyond the sea, for their better improvement'. He conveyed his Yorkshire estate to University College, and also left the College £5,000 to extend their buildings (the present Radcliffe Quadrangle).

The biggest single bequest, however, was £40,000 for the construction of a new library in Oxford, together with £150 a year for a Librarian, £100 a year to purchase books and £100 a year to maintain the building. This came as a surprise to many, for he had not been known

JOHANNES RADCLIFFE MD.
Ob: Nov: 1: 1714.
Æ tat. 64.

LEGAVIT
⎰ *Ad Biblioth: exstruendam 4000ˡⁱᵇ.*
Universitat: Oxon:⎰ *Ad Libros coemendos annuatim 10ˡⁱᵇ.*
⎱ *Pro Salario Bibliothecarij annuatim 15ˡⁱᵇ.*
⎱ *Ad Hospitium Magistri exstruendam 5000ˡⁱᵇ.*
Collegio Universitat ⎰ *duobus Medicis ibidem aliquandiu Commoraturis ann. 600ᵃ*
⎱ *perpetuam Advocationem rectoriæ de Headborne Worthy: et al:*
Insuper Hospitali S: Bartholomæi Lond: annuatim 600ˡⁱᵇ.

3. Frontispiece to *Exequiæ clarissimo viro Johanni Radcliffe*, 1715.

as a bookish man. Indeed, he had made no secret of his preference for direct observation and practical experience. According to one anecdote he was once visited in his college rooms by Ralph Bathurst, Master of Trinity College and a former colleague of the great doctors William Harvey and Thomas Willis. When Bathurst asked Radcliffe where his study was, Radcliffe is said to have pointed to a few vials, a skeleton and a herbal, and replied: 'Sir, this is Doctor Radcliffe's Library.'

Thomas Hearne, for one, was sceptical of Radcliffe's dedication to learning, and charged him with a more worldly motive. 'The Dr [was] but a loose sort of a Man' he noted in his diary on the day of Radcliffe's funeral. 'What he did now for the University was not so much out of a Principle of doing good, as because he could not tell how to dispose of his Money better to gain him a Name after his Death, he being very ambitious of Glory'.

Whatever Radcliffe's reasons were for leaving Oxford such a huge bequest, however, the University authorities were not about to turn it down. They gave him his fine funeral, and the following year the University Press published a collection of poems praising their munificent benefactor. The verses – mostly in Latin, with some contributions in Greek, Hebrew, Arabic and Syriac – were poor stuff, and when Hearne heard about the frontispiece to the volume (fig. 3) he was unimpressed:

> I doubt not but there will be extravagant Commendations in it, not only upon Account of his Benefactions (which indeed are very worthy of Praise) but also on Account of his virtue and Learning, both which I am afraid he wanted as much if not more than anyone yet ever pretended to great Skill in the Faculty of Physick. His Picture is to be in the Front, with Books all about him, which I look upon as absurd, since he was far from being a Bookish Man, and 'tis judged by many that his resolving upon a Library was more the Effect of vain Glory than Love of Books.

The charge of vainglory would be repeated in the coming years, but Radcliffe's motives remain, like most of his inner life, unknowable; and in any case, one does not have to be bookish to found a library. The reality of the legacies listed below the doctor's portrait could hardly be questioned, and in due course the name of this successful and difficult man would be attached to one the most distinctive buildings in the country.

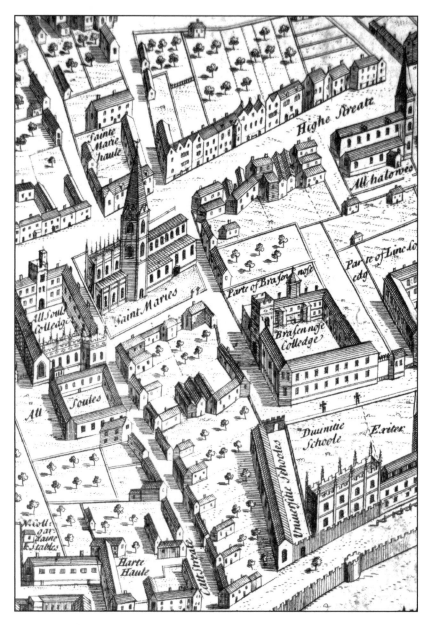

4. Ralph Agas, bird's-eye view of Oxford from the north (detail),
eighteenth-century copy of 1578 original.

The Setting

I F JOHN RADCLIFFE wished to leave his mark on Oxford, then his decision to establish a new Library there was well made. Books had always been the lifeblood of the University. In their early years the colleges and halls had kept a few precious manuscripts in secure chests. As these collections grew in size they had been rehoused in dedicated rooms. They were private libraries, contained within the walls of the colleges and accessible only to their members. The first University Library – that is, a central collection of books that served the organization as a whole, and even scholars from outside Oxford – was confirmed by ordinances of 1412 and situated above Congregation House; the building attached to St Mary's church where University business was conducted. Later in the century the Library moved to a room built above the magnificent new Divinity School, where theology was taught. Next door were the University Schools, where lectures were given on the other parts of the curriculum. Together these few buildings, shown in Ralph Agas's 1578 map of Oxford (fig. 4), made up the University, as the surrounding colleges and halls were – and remain – separately governed communities.

Agas makes no mention in his rubric of a Library above the Divinity School, for by then the room was deserted. Its books had been removed, and even the furniture had been sold. When, a few years later, a retired diplomat called Sir Thomas Bodley, formerly of Merton College, saw this 'great desolate room' he was so dismayed that he proceeded to re-establish the University Library. He saw to the room's refurbishment and purchased a large number of books from home and abroad, providing funds from his own purse and persuading others to support his noble endeavour. 'Bodley's Library', now called the Bodleian, opened its doors to readers at the beginning of the seventeenth century. In 1610–12 Bodley enlarged the library by building an eastern extension, Arts End, at right angles to the existing room. In 1632–7 a further extension was built on to the western side of the Bodleian, mirroring Arts End and giving the building its distinctive 'H' shape, as seen in David

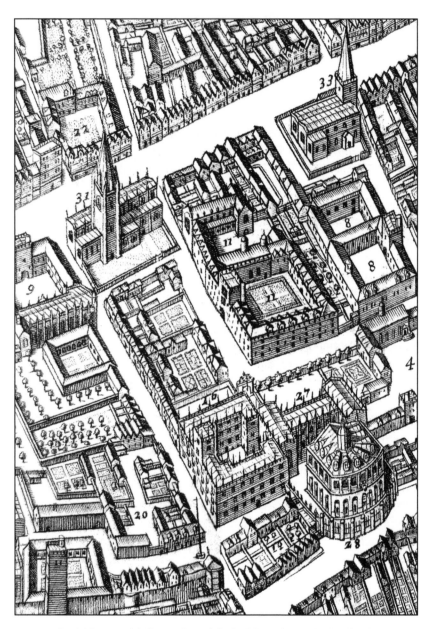

5. David Loggan, bird's-eye view of Oxford from the north (detail), 1675.

Loggan's map of Oxford published in 1675 (fig. 5), where the Library is numbered 27. The ground floor of this second extension, entered from the Divinity School, contained Convocation House, where University business was conducted. The upper floor formed an enlargement of the Bodleian reading room and was known as Selden End, as it housed the large collection of books bequeathed to the Library in 1659 by the lawyer John Selden.

Bodley also helped to instigate, though he never lived to see, the rebuilding between 1613 and 1624 of the University Schools, for its 'ruinous little rooms', as he called them, had become badly neglected. Together the rebuilt Schools and extended Library created a new quadrangle, shown on Loggan's map numbered 16. On the map we can also see St Mary's church (31) and the neighbouring colleges: running along Catte Street to the east are All Souls (9) and Hart Hall (10); to the west are Brasenose (11) and Exeter (4). These institutions surround a central plot of land containing a cluster of small buildings and garden plots – this was the site Radcliffe had settled on for his new library, and he had left money for the existing properties to be purchased and demolished.

Radcliffe thus ensured that his memorial would not only be located at the very heart of the University, but that it would enjoy the proximity of a great existing library, the Bodleian. And happily, his legacy came at a time when Oxford was enjoying a considerable building boom. The University was commissioning new buildings, wealthy patrons were providing the money, and learned college fellows were giving valuable advice at a time of changing tastes: a new acquaintance with ancient and Renaissance architecture, through both books and foreign travel, encouraged Oxford finally to relinquish the Gothic style that had always determined the form of its buildings, and embrace classicism.

Just to the north of the Bodleian in Loggan's engraving, numbered 28, is the rounded shape of the recently completed Sheldonian Theatre. Designed by Christopher Wren and built in 1664–7, this was the first major building in Oxford to observe the classical forms of architecture. It provided a performance space for the various ceremonies of the University, and for inspiration Wren turned to antique models, particularly the Theatre of Marcellus in Rome, which he knew from illustrations in Sebastiano Serlio's *Architettura* (1540). He would shortly leave the city to take up his post as Surveyor of the King's Works, but his promotion of the classical style was continued in Oxford by Radcliffe's two friends, Henry Aldrich and George Clarke.

Aldrich may have been consulted on the design of the graceful new library built at Queen's College in 1692–5. He was certainly responsible for the formal classicism of Peckwater Quadrangle at Christ Church, built in 1706–14. Its spacious rooms met the needs of its intended inhabitants: the wealthy aristocrats and gentleman commoners who now enjoyed Oxford's increasingly secular environment and who expected to be accommodated in the style they were accustomed to in their country houses. Following Aldrich's death Clarke advised the University on most major building projects, and between them the two men ensured that for more than forty years the architectural development of Oxford was both tasteful and well-informed. What is more they could rely on the local services of highly skilled masons and craftsmen.

Whether or not Aldrich and Clarke discussed any of their schemes with Radcliffe, or talked with him more generally about architecture, the doctor would surely have been aware that the University was well-placed to create a building of distinction. He began to explore the idea of a library about two years before his death – that, at least, is when the University became aware of it. It seems that at first he intended it to be an enlargement of the Bodleian. 'I am very glad Dr Radcliffe has given so noble a benefaction to the University', wrote Lord Weymouth to Arthur Charlett at the beginning of 1713, 'which will give them more room, as well as encrease the number of their books.' A letter written by Francis Atterbury, the Dean of Christ Church, to the Bishop of Winchester at the end of the previous year reveals that this enlargement was envisaged as an extension to Selden End, which meant invading the garden of the Bodleian's immediate neighbour, Exeter College. Atterbury explained:

> Doctor Radcliffe's noble design for enlarging the Bodley library goes on. The intended scheme is, to build out from the middle window of the Selden part, a room of ninety feet long, and as high as the Selden part is; and under it to build a library for Exeter College, upon whose ground it must stand. Exeter College has consented, upon condition that not only a library be built for them, but some lodgings also, which must be pulled down to make room for this new design to be rebuilt. The University thinks of furnishing that part of the charge and Dr Radcliffe has readily proffered to furnish the rest; and withal, after he has perfected the building, to give £100 for ever to furnish it with books.

It was a rather elaborate scheme, requiring the goodwill of the fellows of Exeter, the interests of the Bodleian, and University funds; but it was obviously given some serious thought, for there exist a number of fascinating designs for such a library that, although unsigned, have been unanimously attributed to Nicholas Hawksmoor.

Hawksmoor was one of the country's most brilliant architects. He had trained with Sir Christopher Wren, and assisted him on the new Royal Naval Hospital at Greenwich, where he became clerk of works and deputy surveyor. He worked closely with Sir John Vanbrugh on Castle Howard (1700–12) and Blenheim Palace (1705–16), and from 1711 played a central role in a busy programme of new church building in London. His work at Blenheim took him close to Oxford, and he was introduced to the University by George Clarke, with whom he probably became acquainted at Greenwich in 1702–5 when Clarke was secretary to the Admiralty. In 1710 he won an important commission to design a new premises for the University Press on a site next to the Sheldonian Theatre. Constructed in 1712–13 and now referred to as the Clarendon Building, its classical grandeur introduced a monumental approach to the Schools quadrangle and the Bodleian Library. From 1709 Hawksmoor worked with Clarke on the development of the north quadrangle of All Souls and the creation of a new college library, the Codrington, although neither of them would live to see the latter's completion.

Hawksmoor had a deep understanding of historical architectural forms, which he used with great originality and flexibility. He never left England but he was, wrote his obituarist, 'bred a scholar', and he derived his wide knowledge of continental buildings from books. He was also an excellent draughtsman, and a record of his rich and idiosyncratic imagination is provided by the surviving drawings of his many schemes, both realized and unrealized. The scale of his vision for Oxford, and particularly the central University area, is illustrated in a large drawing, dating from around 1713, entitled *Regio Prima Academia Oxoniesis amplificata et exornata* (fig. 6, overleaf). Here Hawksmoor rethinks the city from Cornmarket in the west to Longwall Street in the east, combining the existing buildings with new structures and spaces, and creating a system of vistas, gates and public buildings which recalls the urban planning of ancient and Renaissance Rome. At the centre of the University area is a *Forum Universitatis*; this is balanced by a *Forum Civitatis* at Carfax, complete with a Trajan-style column. On either side of the *Forum Universitatis*

25

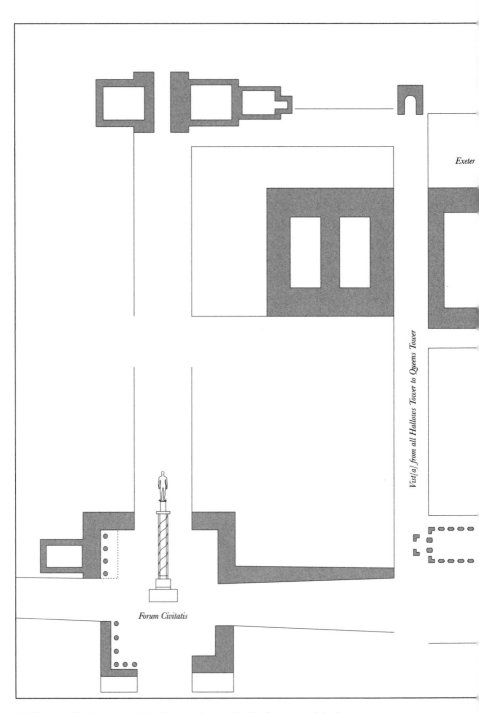

Exeter

Vist[a] from all Hallows Tower to Queens Tower

Forum Civitatis

6. Nicholas Hawksmoor, *Regio Prima*, redrawn detail of *c.* 1713 original.
The entire drawing measures approximately 73 by 161 cm, and continues,
in a much sketchier fashion, to Longwall Street in the east.

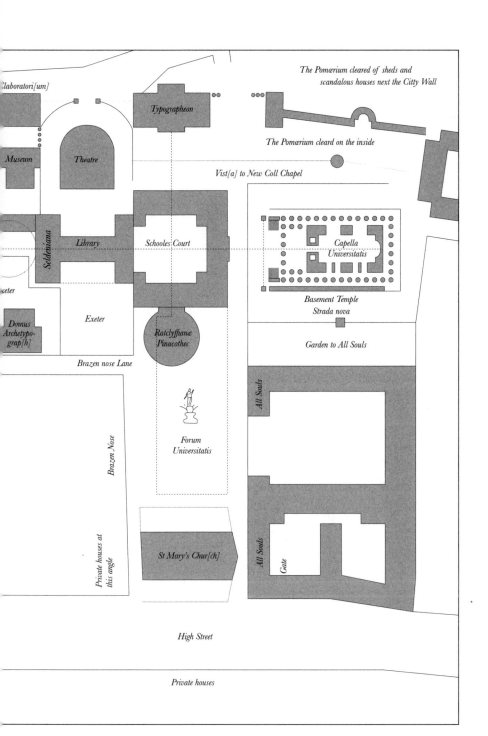

Elaboratori[um]

Typographeon

The Pomœrium cleared of sheds and
scandalous houses next the Citty Wall

The Pomœrium cleard on the inside

Museum

Theatre

Vist[a] to New Coll Chapel

Seldeniana

Library

Schooles Court

Capella
Universitatis

xeter

Basement Temple

Strada nova

Domus
Archetypo-
grap[h]

Exeter

Ratclyffianæ
Pinacothec

Garden to All Souls

Brazen nose Lane

All Souls

Forum
Universitatis

Brazen Nose

Private houses at
this angle

All Souls

St Mary's Chur[ch]

Gate

High Street

Private houses

are a redeveloped All Souls and a rebuilt Brasenose. North of All Souls is an immense new *Capella Universitatis*, imagined as a Greek temple complete with peristyle and grand, stepped entrance, and on an axis with the entrances to the Bodleian and the Schools. The new University printing house can be seen north of the Schools as the *Typographeon*, and there is a house for the University Printer (*Domus Archetypograp*[h]) in Exeter College garden. A building Hawksmoor calls an 'Elaboratorium' has been placed in front of the new University museum, which had been built in 1679–83.

This hugely ambitious – and hugely expensive – scheme was never seriously considered; but it illustrates how Hawksmoor conceived of Radcliffe's Library as one of several new public buildings which, when combined with the existing University structures (the Church, the Library, the Theatre, the printing house), formed a rational and noble academic environment, a place of lectures and books, of religious and secular ceremony

In *Regio Prima* Hawksmoor lightly outlines the circular shape of the Radcliffe Library as an extension to Selden End, and draws it more heavily as an attachment to the south side of the Schools quadrangle. He devised at least five distinct schemes for the former site, of which three propose a rectangular building and two a rotunda, but generally speaking they have a massiveness that appears to justify Hearne's belief that Radcliffe's principal intention was not to serve the world of learning, but to commemorate himself: the proposed buildings certainly have an imposing presence, but they would not have been terribly practical as working libraries. Various classical and later mausolea have been suggested as models, from the Tomb of Caecilia Metella in Rome to Suleiman's mosque in Constantinople, and at home Wren's 1678 design for a mausoleum to Charles I.

One of Hawksmoor's designs for a rotunda is illustrated opposite (fig. 7). The main part of the building is a giant rusticated base of the same height as the adjoining Bodleian. It is surmounted by a drum with arches in alternate bays, and a plain dome with an elegant finial which towers above the existing library. A plan of the first floor (fig. 8) has an outer aisle consisting of five bays and a vestibule. A section drawing of the same design (fig. 9, overleaf) reveals a low basement and above it a vaulted ground floor, quite separate from the rest of the building, which would presumably have served as the new library for Exeter College. A lofty first floor rises up to the roof of an inner dome, decorated

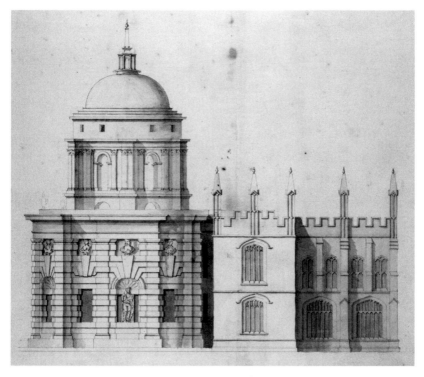

7. Design for a library attached to Selden End of the Bodleian,
probably by Nicholas Hawksmoor; south elevation, *c.* 1713.

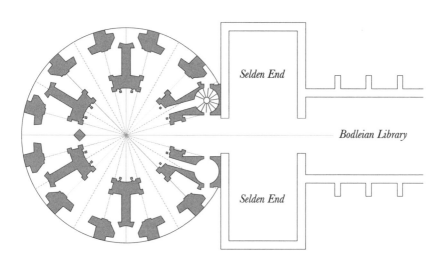

8. First floor plan for the above design, redrawn from
c. 1713 original, probably by Nicholas Hawksmoor

9. Design for a library attached to Selden End of the Bodleian, probably by Nicholas Hawksmoor; section, looking east, *c.* 1713.

10. David Loggan, the Bodleian Library, looking towards Selden End (detail), 1675.

with pilasters and wall niches. Arches lead to an outer corridor, and a gallery is shown above the pilasters. This high classical room, which was presumably entered at the point of the central window in Selden End (fig. 10), would have made a highly dramatic constrast to the low-ceilinged Bodleian, but it is difficult to imagine it as a library space. A statue, busts and urns around the exterior of the building, and further statues in the interior niches below the dome, reinforce the overall impression of a mausoleum.

It is not known why Radcliffe settled on the area to the south of the Schools as the location for his library. Perhaps the agreement that was made with Exeter College for the use of their land fell through. But the new site was certainly more prominent; indeed, as imagined by Hawksmoor as a *Forum Universitatis*, it was the central space of the University. The architect was not the first to envisage such a forum. In 1629 William Laud had proposed clearing the space between the Schools and St Mary's to create a *piazza literaria*. He had the backing of Charles I, who observed that 'certain houses ... take off from the lustre and dignity of the University'. Peter Heylin, Laud's first biographer, later wrote that Laud intended to build on this new space 'a fair and capacious Room, advanced on Pillars; the upper part to serve for Convocations and Congregations ... the lower for a Walk or place of Conference, in which Students of all sorts might confer together.' In the end it proved impossible to secure the necessary leases, but the essence

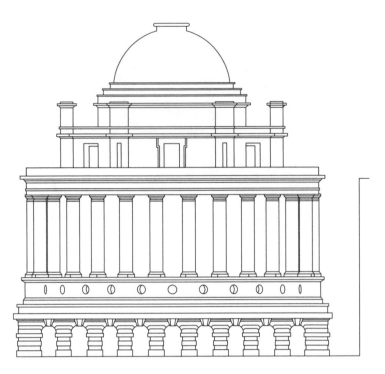

11. Design for a library attached to the south side of the Schools,
redrawn from *c.* 1715 original probably by Nicholas Hawksmoor

of the project was revived with Radcliffe's legacy: his library would be
built in a fine new square and add dignity and lustre to the University.

Two initial schemes by Hawksmoor for a library attached to the south
side of the Schools have survived. The first (fig. 11) proposes a rotunda
on a square base, with a striking peristyle of twenty-eight columns. The
second scheme is shown in plan and in a combined elevation and section on a sheet inscribed by Hawksmoor *Pinacotheca Ratcliffiana anno 1715*
(fig. 12). A main circular building is again surmounted on a square, but
the sides of the base have fewer rusticated arches. The rotunda has a
low circular storey lit by small windows, on which sits a main order of
twenty-four engaged columns. This has both arched and circular windows, and two of the latter are shown with ornate frames, as are the
semi-circular lunettes in the drum above the central rotunda.

The richly imaginative designs Hawksmoor made for Radcliffe's
library around 1713–15 are not rough sketches but finished drawings.
They may have been the subject of conversations between the architect and his regular collaborator, George Clarke. The earlier drawings

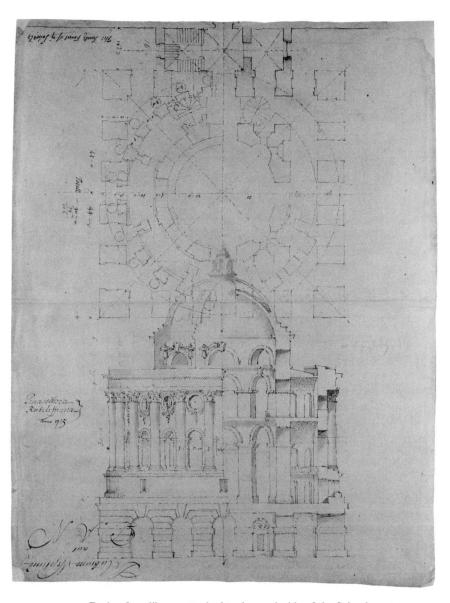

12. Design for a library attached to the south side of the Schools,
probably by Nicholas Hawksmoor, 1715.

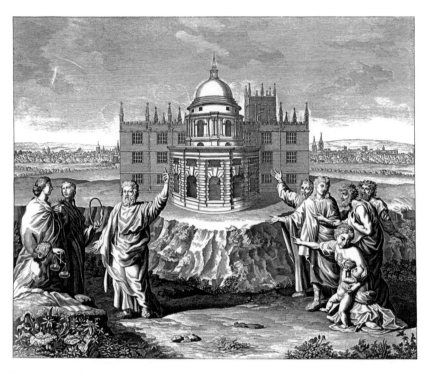

13. The Oxford Almanack, 1716, with an engraving by M. Burghers, depicting a design for the Radcliffe Library.

may have been seen, or even commissioned by Radcliffe himself before his death in December 1714. It would take another thirty-four years to clear the site, build the Library and open it to readers, but Hawksmoor's designs show that the basic conception of a grand mausoleum-type structure standing in an open square was there almost from the beginning.

An engraving in the Oxford Almanack (fig. 13) told members of the University what they might eventually see. Under Clarke's influence these engravings had became a kind of discussion forum for proposed architectural developments in the city. In 1716 the engraver took one of Hawksmoor's Selden End designs (figs 7–9 above) and placed it before the south side of the University Schools, which are shown in isolation against a distant view of Oxford. Classical figures gesture approvingly towards the building. Just over a year after Radcliffe's solemn funeral, Oxford was given a foretaste of his promised library.

⌒ 3 ⌒
The Building

Radcliffe left his estate in the hands of the four distinguished executors he had appointed in his will. Two were prominent politicians: the Right Honourable William Bromley was a former Speaker of the House of Commons and Secretary of State; Sir George Beaumont represented Leicester in Parliament and had served as a Commissioner of the Privy Seal and a Lord of the Admiralty. Like Radcliffe they were Oxford men, high Tories and Jacobites. The third executor, Thomas Sclater Bacon, was a barrister of Gray's Inn and a considerable landowner. The fourth, Anthony Keck, was a banker who had managed the doctor's affairs in the latter part of his life. They quickly set in motion two of Radcliffe's Oxford legacies. In July 1715 the first Radcliffe Fellows were appointed. The following year work commenced on the extension to University College, with George Clarke acting as an advisor; the building was completed in 1719. Work on the library, however, would not start in earnest for another twenty years.

There were two reasons for this long delay. Firstly, Radcliffe's will stipulated that the funds set aside for the library were subject to the life interest of his two sisters, Hannah and Millicent. The latter died the year after Radcliffe, but Hannah lived well into old age, and for years insisted, ultimately without success, that the Executors address themselves not to the library, but to a substantial memorial over Radcliffe's grave in St Mary's church. Secondly, Radcliffe had chosen a difficult site for his new building. He may have left provision in his will for the purchase and demolition of the Catte Street properties, as they were known, but in reality this meant sorting out the complicated freehold and leasehold interests of five colleges (Brasenose, Exeter, Oriel, Magdalene and University), St Mary's and several private individuals.

In early 1717, with George Clarke's assistance, the Executors began informal negotiations with the University over the college properties. They also set about acquiring the privately owned dwellings, and by the end of that year had purchased the freehold of five of them. In 1719 they received a proposal from Brasenose: the college would part with its Catte Street properties (students' lodgings, a coach house and stables, a brewery, two gardens), but only if the Radcliffe Executors were to purchase for them several properties they desired just to the south of their quadrangle. To consider this offer, the Executors had a plan made showing the various properties and their owners (a version of this map, with the superimposed outline of the proposed library, was later engraved and published for its historic interest (fig. 14). In the summer of 1720 Bromley and Beaumont, encouraged by the soaring value of Radcliffe stock in the South Sea Company, told their fellow Executors that they were 'of opinion that since the Doctor's estate is so much increas'd, that it will be proper to purchase the rest of the houses and ground in Oxon for building the Library as soon as conveniently may be'. They even made a quick list of the 'ablest Architects': Sir Christopher Wren, Sir John Vanbrugh, Sir James Thornhill, Thomas Archer, Nicholas Hawksmoor, John James and James Gibbs. Then the South Sea Bubble collapsed, greatly reducing the Executors' immediate funds, and there is no evidence that any of the architects were approached that year.

It also became clear that both St Mary's and the Colleges were prevented by law from selling their properties or granting long leases. To resolve this, a petition was presented to Parliament in 1721 for a bill enabling the sale, either to the Radcliffe Executors or their heirs, of any college or church property, or private property held in trust, 'which by them shall be judged and deemed necessary and convenient for building the said Library, and for making the Approach thereunto convenient and beautiful'. Otherwise, the petition warned, Radcliffe's benefaction would be rendered ineffectual, 'to the great Prejudice of the said University, detriment to Learning and Discouragement of the like pious and publick Benefactions for the future'. An Act of Parliament was soon passed, and although there was still much further discussion to be had with the church and colleges, it did allow the Executors to acquire, almost immediately, the last of the private properties: a house and garden adjoining the south side of the Schools Quadrangle.

There matters rested until February 1733, when the house adjoining the Schools was demolished, 'for fear of a chimney's setting fire to the Schools; and to open a passage to the Schools.' In March the following year the surviving Executors (Sir George Beaumont, Thomas Bacon and Anthony Keck) and new Trustees (William Bromley Jr. and Edward Harley, later the 3rd Earl of Oxford) informed the Vice-Chancellor of

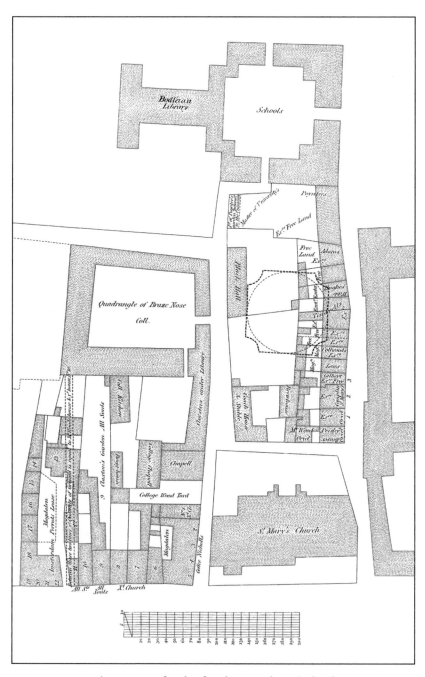

14. A 1743 copy of a plan first drawn up in 1718, showing
the properties in Catte Street and south of Brasenose College.

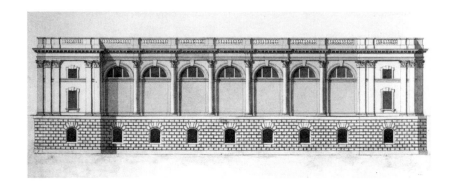

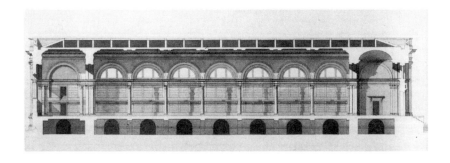

15–17. Designs for a rectangular library between the Schools and St Mary's Church,
probably by James Gibbs; elevations and section, *c.* 1730s.

their determination to reach an agreement with the colleges over the remaining Catte Street properties, for they were 'desirous to compleat Dr Radcliffe's benefaction with the utmost Expedition'. The subsequent negotiations were laborious, so in the meantime thought was given to the design of the library, and in 1734–5 at least two architects, Nicholas Hawksmoor and James Gibbs, were asked to submit plans.

Hawksmoor's high reputation and early association with the project made him an obvious candidate. Gibbs was similarly well-regarded. He had designed a number of churches and monuments in London and elsewhere, and published two books: *Book of Architecture* (1728) and *Rules for Drawing the Several Parts of Architecture* (1732). He also had local connections: in 1719–26 he had built an important country house in Oxfordshire, Ditchley Park, and he enjoyed a close association with the Earls of Oxford. Of the other 'ablest Architects' listed by the Executors in 1720, Wren, Vanbrugh and Thornhill were all dead.

Gibbs proposed a rectangular, two-storied building which, at 200 feet long by 100 feet wide, would have filled most of the space created by the demolition of the Catte Street properties. The design illustrated opposite (figs. 15–17) has a rusticated basement, with a long central range of arches and three-quarter composite columns, and projecting end wings with pilasters. Two rows of columns divide the first-floor interior into aisles and a central nave. The aisles are divided into seven bays, and the walls contain two tiers of books divided by a central gallery. High windows above the bookcases provide light in a manner similar to Wren's superb library at Trinity College, Cambridge. It is a very practical solution, offering plenty of space for books, but it does lack the impact of Hawksmoor's rotunda schemes.

Hawksmoor, meanwhile, made a number of revisions but no radical changes to his design of 1715 (fig. 12, p. 33). His final thoughts on the library are to be found in the wooden scale model made by the London master joiner John Smallwell Jr in 1734–5 at the request of the Radcliffe Trustees (see colour pls II & III). The existence of Hawksmoor's last design in such an expensive form (the model cost more than £87 to make) suggests that this was the scheme favoured by the Trustees. The massiveness of the square base has been lessened with concave corners; the main rotunda has fewer columns, and now has single pedimented windows alternating with niches; but the building still resembles a mausoleum: urns fill the basement niches, and there are indications that least one niche in the main rotunda would have contained a statue.

The model, which can be taken to pieces to reveal the layout of the interior, was shown to members of the University for their comments. It was clearly different from the library depicted in the 1716 Almanack (fig. 13, p. 34), which confused some, but generally the response was favourable. There was, however, some concern about its location. In January 1737 Sir George Beaumont's relative William Busby told the antiquary and collector Richard Rawlinson:

> From Oxford I hear the model for the Library is much liked but the only objections are that the design of a communication with the other Library will not bear. The passage thro' the Schools, if continued will lye too near Brazen Nose, whereas according to the model it should go thro' the center, so that the scheme for a thorough view from the Printing House to St Mary's will be impractical.

With great effect, Hawksmoor had positioned the printing house on the north-south axis of the Schools. In his *c.* 1713 plan of the city (fig. 6, p. 26) he had put the Radcliffe Library on the same axis, and it can immediately be seen that this meant tucking it into the north-west corner of the new square, uncomfortably close to Exeter and Brasnenose Colleges. In one plan Hawksmoor attempts to solve this problem with a T-shaped linking structure (fig. 18); the Trustees' plan of the Catte Street properties (fig. 14, p. 37), by contrast, shows his building as a central, free-standing building. The library could either follow the vista through the printing house and the Schools, or provide a focal point for the square – it could not do both.

The library would probably have been built according to the model, had not Hawksmoor died in March 1736 after a long and painful illness. On his death the commission passed to James Gibbs, who made a number of revisions to Hawksmoor's scheme. Radcliffe's sister Hannah also died that year, aged well over 80, and this finally released the funds intended for the library. In 1736–7 the Trustees concluded their negotiations with St Mary's and the colleges and purchased the remaining properties on the Catte Street site. After a twenty-year wait, they were at last ready to start on the demolition and building work.

On 4 March 1737 Gibbs attended a Trustees meeting, together with two master masons, William Townesend of Oxford and Francis Smith of Warwick. Smith had worked with Gibbs on Ditchley Hall.

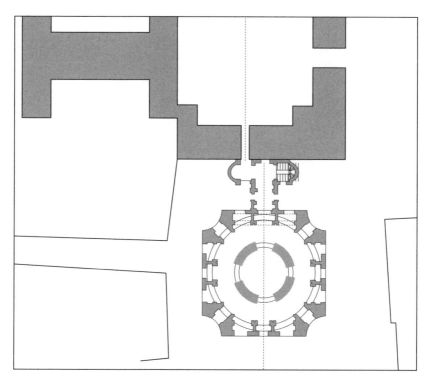

18. Plan showing a library attached to the south side of the Schools,
probably by Nicholas Hawksmoor, redrawn from *c.* 1734 original.

Townesend was from a dynasty of Oxford masons, and had a hand in virtually every building of importance built in the city between 1710 and 1740, including the new printing house, the north quadrangle of All Souls and the Radcliffe extension to University College. This hugely experienced Oxford craftsman began to prepare the hard Headington stone in which the lower part of the library would be built, and at a meeting on 1 April looked over, and approved, the 'great improvements' Gibbs had made.

It was agreed at the April meeting that Gibbs' designs should be engraved on copper 'and given to the Heads of Houses in Oxford and the noblemen there' so that any objections could be raised before work started. Six hundred sets of five large engravings by George Vertue, in a blue wrapper headed *Bibliotheca Radcliffiana*, were printed off and distributed: 100 for the Vice Chancellor, twelve for the Chancellor, twenty to Gibbs, twelve for Charles Pryor (the secretary to the Trustees) and the

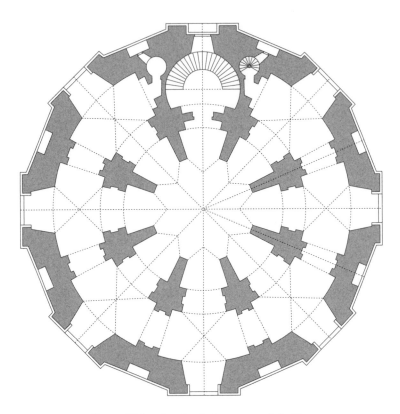

19. James Gibbs, plan for the basement of the library,
redrawn from 1737 engraving.

remainder for the Trustees themselves. The first engraving shows the
library in the position it enjoys today: in the centre of the new square
without any attachment to the Schools. The next two plates presented
detailed plans of the 'rustic basement' and the main floor. They revealed
that Gibbs had replaced Hawksmoor's square basement and rotunda
with a single sixteen-sided polygon. The two floors are each divided
into seven bays and an internal horseshoe staircase obviates the need
for a projecting entrance to the reading room on the first floor, thereby
preserving the sense of a purely circular building. Dotted lines in the
basement plan (fig. 19) traced the shape of its vault, and a balustrade in
the first-floor plan indicated the presence of a gallery level.

The fourth and fifth engravings provided an elevation and a section
view of the library (Gibbs' finely shaded original drawings are illustrated

42

overleaf, figs 20 and 21). Here one could see that Hawksmoor's single columns had been replaced by twinned Corinthian pilasters. Along the main drum an upper and lower window alternate with a lower window and upper niche. The urns have been removed from the basement and placed on the balustrade above the main drum and around the cupola. The elevation showed part of the basement vaulting and revealed that it had four open entrances. Massive pillars and wide arches divide the reading room into bays, and the tall bookshelves are divided into two tiers by a gallery. Both the dome and lantern are shown made of stone, and the inside of the dome is elaborately ornamented.

On 17 May 1737 the foundation stone of the library was laid in the newly created space between St. Mary's church and the University Schools, a space that had already become known as Radcliffe Square. A copper plaque containing the date and the names of the Vice-Chancellor, the Radcliffe Trustees and the architect was added to the stone. The ceremony, complete with Latin oration, was attended by the Vice-Chancellor, the Doctors, Proctors and Masters of the University, and the five Radcliffe Trustees. Radcliffe's original four Executors were now dead (the last, Sir George Beaumont, had died just six weeks before the foundation ceremony). Of the Trustees, Edward Harley had been elected in 1732. The others had all been elected in the previous two months: Lord Charles Noel Somerset (later the 4th Duke of Beaufort), the Rt Hon John Verney, Master of the Rolls, Sir Walter Wagstaff Bagot MP and Edward Smith MP.

A clerk of works, Thomas Jersey, was appointed, and construction work commenced. By March 1738 the fabric had reached as far as the top of the basement piers, and it was at this point that Gibbs clearly began to worry about the ultimate success of such a prominent building, a building on which the architectural integrity of the University, and his own reputation rested. On 10 March he sent a long letter to Somerset. He allowed that Townesend and Smith were 'able and skill-full artists', but felt nevertheless that he should keep in close touch with the building: 'My Lord, all building should have three Essential qualities, use, strength, and beauty. There is none fitter to consider these better than your Architect, yet this he cannot do, unless he sees the building as it advances.' The library was not, Gibbs wrote, like a counting house, seen by few (none of them expert) and easy to patch up if a mistake is made in the building or the decoration:

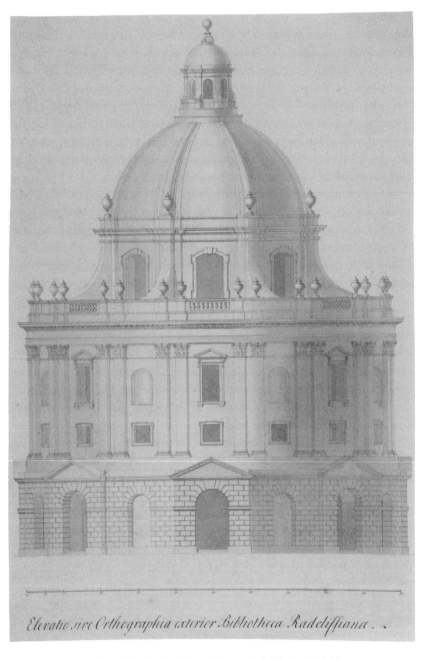

20. James Gibbs, *Elevatio sive Orthographia exterior Bibliotheca Radcliffiana*, 1737.

Sectio sive Orthographia interior Bibliotheca Radcliffiana.

21. James Gibbs, *Sectio sive Orthographia interior Bibliotheca Radcliffiana*, 1737.

This is a Regular Ornamental pile of Building, formed according to the just rules of Architecture, and of due Symmetry and Proportion, and if finished as it should be, will be one of the finest buildings in England. This is a publick Building seen by all sorts of people who come to Oxford from different parts of the World, and is to be applauded or condemned by the best Judges according as it is executed …

Gibbs reminded Somerset that as the building was constructed in stone, mistakes could not be rectified or plastered over; things had to be right first time. Accordingly, on 14 July 1738 he signed an agreement with the Trustees whereby he would be paid £100 a year for 'directing and supervising the Building of the Radcliffe Library and drawing all plans that shall be necessary for completing the work and corresponding with the Builders and going down four times in every year to see the Building'.

It is clear from Gibbs' letter that, at this stage at least, his concern was with the beauty and classical correctness of the building; he makes no mention of its practical use as a library. This emphasis on ornament was remarked on in August 1738 by Rawlinson's friend William Brome, who was shown a set of engravings by Edward Harley: 'by the pictures I thought 'twould be a decoration, if not much use to the University.'

The engravings Brome was looking at were, in fact, out of date, for Gibbs was making late changes. He had replaced the pilasters around the drum with three-quarter columns, lowered the entablature round the base of the dome, added ribbing to the dome itself and enclosed the main staircase. The Trustees, their patience perhaps wearing thin, sought an assurance from Gibbs that he had no further changes to make, and in March 1740 ordered George Vertue to make a new set of engravings. By this time the walls of the library had risen to the level of the balustrade above the main order. There had been changes on the site: Francis Smith had died in April 1738; William Townesend had grown infirm and would die in September that year; but they had been succeeded by their capable sons, William Smith and John Townesend. Apart from a small delay caused by an outbreak of smallpox, work continued uninterrupted through the autumn and winter.

Then, in February 1741, main construction was halted. Townesend and Smith were instructed 'not to go on with any part of the building or cupulor till further directions from the Trustees'. As they had already completed 5 feet 8 inches of the dome they submitted a bill for this work. The Trustees asked the masons 'to send a distinct account of the ... work done of the doom [*sic*]' and further, 'to send a positive answer by whose order they began to build the dome of stone'. There had apparently been a breakdown in communication: the Trustees had been advised by Gibbs that it would be better to build in the dome in wood and lead, rather than stone, but for some reason this had not been passed on to the masons. The reason for this confusion is not known, but the Trustees eventually accepted the mason's bill and in April ordered that the existing stone work should remain, 'Mr Gibbs being of opinion that the timber work will be as strong and substantial as if it were taken down again.' The switch from stone to timber was not simple, however. There exists a sizeable bill from Smith and Townesend for 'Masons Work done in taking down part of the Stone Work of the Dome, and levelling the same, and taking out the Inside Ribbs for the Carpenters to fix the Principals, and walling up the same'. All this was not completed until the end of November 1742, so the work on the dome was delayed for more than a year as a result of the change in material.

It is not recorded why Gibbs changed his mind about the material. Perhaps he doubted the local masons' ability to conshtruct a stone dome that wouldn't collapse. A scale model had been made in stone (it now tops a summerhouse in the garden of St Giles House in Oxford) but the real thing was another matter, for no one in England had ever built such a structure. Gibbs had expressed his anxiety about 'the support of the Tholus or Cupola, which likewise is to be of stone' in his letter to Somerset:

> no small thought is required to consider it well, both as to its Centring, and forming its Hemesphere, its diameter being 48 feet, and to proportion its Weight so that it may not crash its legs, or be damaged by the insufficiency of its Buttresses and Crampings.

By March 1743 the timber frame of the dome had been constructed and covered with 63 tons of lead. Once the balustrade and lantern had been completed the workers started to dismantle the scaffolding, in the process of which there was a fatal accident: part of the scaffolding collapsed, killing two and injuring others. On 18 March the Trustees asked Townesend for the names of those killed and injured, and in April paid £20 'for the Benefitt of Mary Hearn and her children whose husband was killed by the fall of the scaffold at the Library.'

The exterior of the building was now almost finished, so attention turned to the interior furnishing and decoration. The finest craftsmen and artisans were engaged – painters, plasterers, carpenters, plumbers, pavers, iron workers, wood carvers, locksmiths – their progress somewhat slowed in the winter months by a strict instruction from the Trustees that for reasons of safety no work could be done by candlelight. In March 1745 a marble statue of John Radcliffe was commissioned from the Flemish sculptor Michael Rysbrack, whose first completed work after his arrival in England in 1720 had been a monument to the poet Matthew Prior designed by James Gibbs. Now one the foremost sculptors in England, Rysbrack had recently carved the monument to Sir Isaac Newton in Westminster Abbey (1731) and the memorial to the 1st Duke of Marlborough at Blenheim Palace (1733). For his statue of Radcliffe he worked from a vivid portrait by Sir Godfrey Kneller showing the doctor, splendidly dressed and wigged, in his prosperous sixties (colour pl. 1). It had once been the property of George Clarke, who on his death in 1736, had bequeathed it to the University, stipulating that it be placed in Radcliffe's library, 'when built'. Today it hangs at the top of the main staircase of the library.

Rysbrack's six-foot statue was completed in 1747 and hoisted into its place of honour, a pedimented niche above the main entrance to the library. 'As to Radcliffe's Library', wrote Thomas Hunt, Laudian Professor of Arabic, to Rawlinson that March, 'the outside and area are now entirely finished, and I believe the Inside wants but little of being so.' With the building all but complete, Gibbs published a finely produced book of engravings, *Bibliotheca Radcliviana: or a short description of the Radcliffe Library at Oxford*. In his introductory text he graciously thanked the Radcliffe Trustees for their 'Unanimity, Integrity, and Candor' and for the promptness of their payments, and gave a concise account of Radcliffe's life and the history of the project since his death. He named the Radcliffe Executors and Trustees who had been involved over the years, and the craftsmen who had worked on the building. The copper plates comprised portraits of Radcliffe and Gibbs himself, and twenty-one architectural engravings by Paul Fourdrinier scrupulously copied from Gibbs' careful drawings. The 'Plans, Uprights, Sections, and Ornaments' reproduced the essential features of the outside and inside of the building, and were prefaced by short explanations from Gibbs. (A selection of the plates and explanations are provided as an appendix to this book.)

Bibliotheca Radcliviana is an exercise in self-promotion, a meticulous record of a building which, Gibbs pointed out more than once, had been designed according to correct classical principles. As a library it was highly distinctive, indeed unique. In 1675 Sir Christopher Wren had drawn a design for a circular reading room at Trinity College, Cambridge which had never been realized. A round library had subsequently been built at Wolfenbuettel, near Brunswick in Germany, in 1706–10, but the Radcliffe Library was the first such building in Britain.

The first visitors to the library would have entered from the basement. At a time when libraries were usually situated on the first floor to protect their contents from damp this basement served a practical purpose. It was not, however, some dingy undercroft, but an attractive, airy porch in which respectable pedestrians could wander, gather or take shelter, very much like the 'place of Conference' William Laud had imagined a century earlier (colour pl. vi). Its seven arches were filled with fine iron gates by Robert Bakewell of Derby (appendix: pl. viii). Four were fixed; the other three could be opened, but were always locked at night 'to enclose and preserve that Place from being a lurking Place for Rogues ... or any other ill Use'. Radcliffe's coat of arms were displayed in the centre of the vault and the floor was paved with a geometrical design (appendix: pl. xvi).

On the north side of the basement was a doorway leading to a grand staircase with a balustrade of ornamental ironwork, which would have taken the first visitors to the great room above (appendix: pl. xv). This main space was magnificent, but early visitors could be forgiven for thinking that they were in a centrally planned church rather than a library. The centre of the floor, then free of furniture, was paved with Portland stone intermixed with red Swedish or Bremen, on which light fell from the high windows and the lantern of the cupola. The visitors would at once have been impressed by the room's defining feature, the great circular arcade, its seven wide arches resting on massive piers with twinned Ionic pilasters (colour pl. xii). A balustraded gallery, reached by way of two small spiral staircases built into the wall next to the main staircase, encircled almost the entire room. Above the door stood Rysbrack's statue of Radcliffe (colour pl. xi; appendix: pl. xii), in academic dress and accompanied by a serpent, a symbol of medicine.

Looking further upwards, the visitors would doubtless have admired the superb cartouches carved in stone in the spandrels between the arches, the elaborate cornice, the a row of windows acting like a clerestory in a church, and finally the dome, lavishly decorated in finely coloured plaster (colour pl. x; appendix: pls xviii & xix). The plaster decoration, one of the glories of the building, was the work of Giuseppe Artari, an exceptionally accomplished Swiss stuccoist who had previously worked with Gibbs on a number of projects, including Ditchley Park. Artari had two collaborators: Charles Stanley, originally from Denmark, and Thomas Roberts, a resident of Oxford who also did outstanding work in Christ Church library and the senior common room of St John's College.

The woodwork was by John Phillips: not only the flooring and windows, but the thirty mahogany seats, the double-sided, sloping reading desks (shown as square outlines in the plans opposite, fig. 22), and the mahogany bookcases with wire-meshed fronts and adjustable, slotted shelving. Extra ornamentation was added by a specialist woodcarver, William Linnell. The bookcases stood against the outer walls of the building behind the arcade, and were curved to fit the walls' circular shape. Over the years the University had observed wider trends in the arrangement of library books. In its medieval libraries the volumes had been chained to lecterns, which were arranged in rows down the sides of rectangular rooms; low windows between the lecterns provided the necessary light. As collections grew, the lecterns were replaced with bookcases, or presses, which were placed between the windows at right-angles to the walls, creating alcoves. Incorporated into the bookcases were desks at which readers could consult the chained books. The Bodleian and the Merton College Library were early examples of this 'alcove system'. In a final development, volumes were stored in tall bookcases placed flat against the walls in the manner familiar today. These bookcases could stretch from floor to ceiling, and access to the upper shelves was provided by a gallery which divided the bookcases into two tiers. The Arts End extension to the Bodleian (seen in the foreground of fig. 10, p. 31) was the first English example of the 'wall system'. The bookcases in the Radcliffe Library are also arranged according to this system, but their division into bays, each with their sloping desks and central windows, recall the earlier alcove and lectern systems (appendix: pl. xiv). Alas, the early visitors to the library would only have seen empty shelves for, as discussed in the next chapter, it would be some time before they contained appreciable quantities of books.

Only a privileged few would have had access to the main floor of the library, but anyone passing between the University Schools and

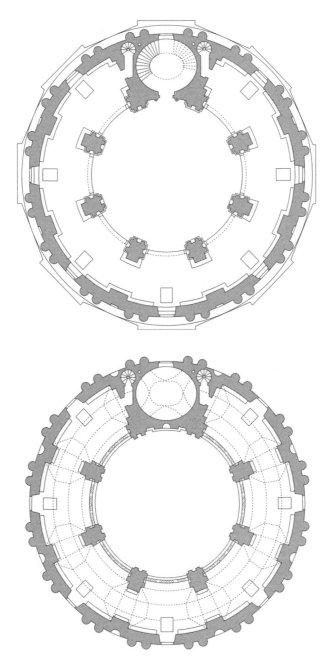

22. James Gibbs, plans of the first floor and gallery
of the library, redrawn from 1747 engraving.

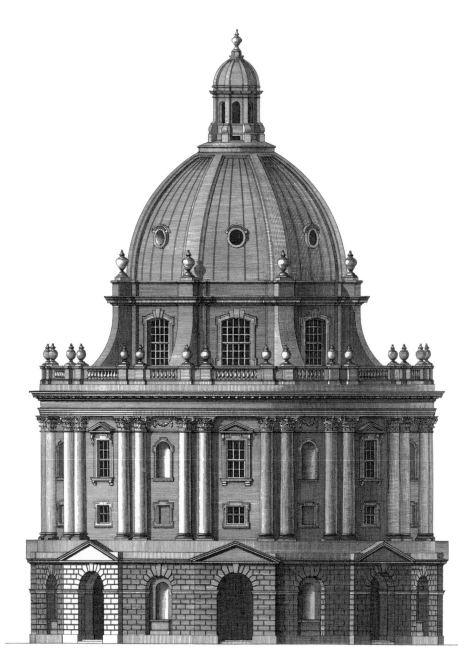

23. P. Fourdrinier after James Gibbs, *The Geometrical Upright of the outside of the Library*, 1747.

St Mary's church would have been treated to a view of the great domed rotunda that dominated the new square and at the same time successfully complemented the Gothic style of its immediate neighbours. Gibbs had received his early training in Rome,where he had studied under Carlo Fontana, who had been a pupil of Gianlorenzo Bernini, and the final form of the Radcliffe Library owed much to his first-hand experience of the numerous domed churches of Renaissance and Baroque Rome. There is no single prototype, but its similarity to Bramante's Tempietto in the cloister of San Pietro in Montorio has often been noticed.

The fifth engraving in *Bibliotecha Radcliviana* (fig. 23) shows the architect's skilful employment of classical forms. 'This shews the Geometrical Upright of the Outside of the Building', wrote Gibbs in his explanation to the plate,

> being of the *Corinthian* Order, with its balustrade and Vases a-top. This Order has all the Members of its Entablature properly enriched, and the Capitals, and Festoons betwixt them neatly carved, all the Windows and Niches are regularly dressed; and its middle Part adorned with a handsome Cupola and Lanthorn covered with Lead, the whole erected on a Rustic Basement; the plan of which is a regular Polygon of sixteen Sides.

The syncopated rhythms created by the alternating arches, columns, niches, windows and buttresses enliven the building's regular shape; the massiveness of the rusticated base, built in hard Headington Stone, is lightened by the more decorative rotunda it supports, made from contrasting ochre coloured Burford stone (since refaced; see colour pl. IX).

With the completion of the Radcliffe Library the heart of Oxford University assumed its final architectural form. This superb Baroque edifice ended the building boom that had been initiated in Oxford in the 1660s by Wren's Sheldonian Theatre, and which had transformed the medieval character of the city.

In the spring of 1748 the Radcliffe Trustees appointed a porter, the splendidly named Pudsey Mussendine, to look after the building. They gave him a salary of £20 per annum, a suit of livery (to be renewed every two years), and a silver-headed staff bearing Radcliffe's coat of arms. He took over from an impoverished servant, Ralph Pettit, who for the last two years had been acting as a caretaker, keeping the building clean and clear of rubbish.

The Trustees then considered the vital question of the first Radcliffe Librarian. There had been speculation about this desirable post ever since John Radcliffe's lifetime. 'I am now every minute in expectation of seeing Dr Radcliffe', Thomas Allen of University College had told Thomas Hearne in the summer of 1713. 'The last time I had that happiness, he told me he designed to make you his Library-keeper and to send you abroad to buy bookes for his library. I assured him he could not send a more faithfull, skillfull and industrious person on that errand and thanked him for that favour.' Shortly after Radcliffe's death Browne Willis wrote to Hearne: 'A godson of Dr Radcliffe's who called on me last week told me you might if you asked for it and wrote a letter to Dr Mead secure to yourself the libarian's place of Dr Radcliffe's library which is worth 150£ per annum though I have no notion of any salary till there is a library etc.' But Radcliffe had not named Hearne in his will, and so Hearne assumed he had changed his mind. 'I heard of Dr. Radcliffe's Design of constituting me his Librarian some time agoe', he told Rawlinson at the beginning of 1714, 'and I sent the Dr my thanks. I will not pretend to guess how he came to alter his intent.'

In 1722 the various heads of Oxford's colleges and halls met to discuss a recent benefaction to the University. They debated whether it should be put towards the salary of the Librarian of the Bodleian. Dr William King, Principal of St Mary Hall, suggested that the posts of Bodley's and Radcliffe's Librarian could be combined. Hearne recorded the subsequent exchange:

> since 'twas very probable that the same Man hereafter would be Librarian of Dr Radcliff's Library as well as Bodley's, then 'twould be a most noble Thing of itself, Dr Radcliffe's Salary being £150 per annum. They said they were to be distinct Librarians. But, says the Dr, suppose the Bodleian Library hereafter … should be a Man of Worth, and be recommended by some great Man or Men above to be Librarian also to the Radcliffe Library, I suppose there will be a Complyance to such a Request, and no one of you the Heads will be against it. To this they could say nothing.

And nothing further happened until June 1737, a month after the foundation stone of the library had been laid, when an ambitious junior librarian at the Bodleian named Francis Wise was advised by his friends to pursue 'an affair, having more interest and profit in it, than learning'. For the next ten years Wise lobbied hard to become the first Radcliffe Librarian, and when the rather formidable selection panel (the Archbishop of Canterbury, the Lord Chancellor, the Chancellor of Oxford, the Bishop of London, the Bishop of Winchester, the two principle secretaries of state, and the two Lord Chief Justices) met in the Prince's Chamber in the House of Lords on 10 May 1748, he was duly elected, but only by a single vote.

At a meeting the following February, the Radcliffe Trustees formally recorded that they had fulfilled their duties relating to the Library. The secretary ticked them off in the minutes: '£40,000 given for building a Library at Oxford which has all been laid out and the Library compleated and the tradesmen all paid. £150 per annum to the Librarian. £100 per annum to buy books. £100 per annum for repairing the Library.' There only remained the official opening. It had been planned for the previous year, but been postponed on account of drunken disturbances in Oxford. Jacobite students had walked through the streets shouting toasts to the Young Pretender, and there had been a physical altercation with the Revd Richard Blacow, a Whiggish Canon of Windsor. The Trustees, who were all Tories and Jacobites, had no doubt feared that in such a climate the opening might have become an occasion for political agitation and riotous behaviour. So they had waited.

Dr Radcliffe's library was officially opened on Thursday, 13 April 1749. The splendid ceremonies, which lasted from Tuesday to Friday, were described in detail by a Hebrew scholar, Benjamin Kennicott. 'Almost all the Lodging in Oxford had been engaged for some time,' he wrote, 'and on Monday Night [9 April] the Town began to fill.' A programme of the forthcoming events had been published, together with a strict request that decorum should be maintained throughout. On Tuesday three of the Trustees, the Duke of Beaufort, the Earl of Oxford and Edward Smith, arrived to the welcome of 'almost all the Bells in the City', and were entertained at dinner by Mr Rowney, one of the City Members. The remaining Trustees, Sir Walter Bagot and Sir Watkin Williams Wynn, arrived the following day, and at 11 o'clock that morning, 'the Whole University being seated in the [Sheldonian] Theatre in their Robes, and according to their Standing', honorary degrees were awarded, including a Master of Arts to James Gibbs. The Trustees were then entertained at dinner by the Vice-Chancellor, and at four in the afternoon there was a performance of Handel's oratorio *Esther*. It was managed by William Hayes, the Professor of Music, 'who had got together from London and Places about forty Voices and fifty Instruments', and performed to an audience, Kennicott reckoned, 'of about 15,000, and the only part anchored was the fine Coronation Anthem, God save the King'.

On Thursday morning the senior members of the University and the Radcliffe Trustees proceeded from St Mary's Church to the library, where the Duke of Beaufort, on behalf of the Trustees, presented the keys to the building to the Vice-Chancellor, who gave a short speech of thanks. The main event took place in the Sheldonian later that day. After the award of further honorary degrees, and 'a flourish of Musick, which preceded and succeeded every Article of Business', two orations were delivered. The first of the Public Orators appointed for the occasion, Dr Lewis, spoke for about half an hour 'in a manner so elegant and Masterly as did great honour to the Names of Dr Radcliffe, the Trustees and himself'. Then, 'amidst the Thunder of the Theatre', the second orator, Dr William King, rose from his seat. He spoke for nearly an hour, seemingly from memory, but, commented Kennicott, ''tis said his Son sat behind him to prompt him, and to hold his Lemon.' King was a famous orator, and knowing this would be his last oration he had, Kennicott observed, 'resolved to go off gloriously, and to speak, this once, with all the Spirit of a Dying Patriot.' An arch Tory and Jacobite, King ended with a rousing description of 'the present unhappy Situation of Oxford, and the miserable State of poor Great Britain, and concluded, since all Other Endeavours to save this Nation from Corruption and —— were found ineffectual, we shou'd betake our Selves to Prayer.' A Handel anthem was then sung, and the Vice-Chancellor concluded by thanking the Radcliffe Trustees. As the assembly left the theatre, to 'the Loud Acclamations of the Young Part of the University', there was a further burst of politics: several among the youthful crowd were 'absurd enough' to cheer the name of Sir Watkin, a renowned Jacobite, and hiss the name of the Rector of Exeter College, a Whig. The day ended with a performance of another Handel oratorio, *Sampson*.

On Friday members of the University gathered once more in the Sheldonian. Further degrees were awarded, then Dr Henry Brooke, Regius Professor of Civil Law, and a Whig, gave a speech criticizing Dr King's oration of the previous day: 'He hop'd', reported Kennicott, 'that such a Concourse of venerable persons had been now assembled, not *from a political principle but the Love of Learning*, and was therefore sorry their Ears had been so abused with Reflections on the Misery of the

24. G. Vertue, depiction of the opening of the Radcliffe Library
on 13 April 1749, for the Oxford Almanack, 1751.

Nation.' The four days' of ceremony then concluded with a performance of a final Handel oratorio – *Messiah*. Kennicott put the total cost
at around £20,000.

Two years later, in 1751, the handing over ceremony in the library
was depicted in the Oxford Almanack (fig. 24). An accompanying
explanation read: 'On the Area are Dr Radcliffe's five Trustees, *viz*.
His Grace the Duke of Beaufort, The Right Honourable The Earl of
Oxford, Sir Walter Wagstaff Bagot Baronet, Sir Watkin Williams Wynn
Baronet, and Edward Smith Esquire, Delivering the Keys to *Alma-
Mater*. ... On the right Side of *Alma-Mater* are four *Genii*, representing
Physick, Anatomy, Chemistry and Botany. The Personages on each Side
and in the Gallerys, are Spectators supposed to be present at the Said
Solemnity.' And looking paternally over the proceedings, from his niche
above the entrance, is Dr Radcliffe himself.

25. Parr after W. Halfpenny, view of the Radcliffe Library,
looking south from the University Schools, *c.* 1750.

⤙ 4 ⤚
A New Library

THE FIRST ENGRAVING of the Radcliffe Library was published soon after the opening, and dedicated to the Chancellor, Vice-Chancellor and Heads of the Colleges and Halls of Oxford University (fig. 25). Gowned academics and smartly dressed ladies and gentlemen stand before the spectacular new building, which rises high above its neighbours at the centre of a spacious piazza, obscuring the Gothic spire of St Mary's to the south. 'The most magnificent Structure in *Oxford* is the new publick Library', the travel writer Thomas Salmon had written in the later stages of its construction; but he did wonder how it would be filled, Radcliffe having left just '100*l. per Annum* to buy Books for this capacious Edifice'. Perhaps, Salmon conjectured, 'he expected the Books would one Day be removed from the *Bodleian* Library to replenish this'. Hearne had suggested that the Library was motivated by a wish for posthumous glory. Thirty years later Salmon reported that the city's inhabitants held a similar opinion: 'whatever the Doctor designed or expected from his laying out 40,000 *l.* in building one Room, I find a great many People of Opinion that he intended to perpetuate his Memory by it, and therefore give it the Name of *Ratcliff's Mausolaeum.*'

Few however denied the Library's beauty as a piece of architecture, and over the next few years the Radcliffe Trustees undertook improvements to its immediate surroundings. A high wall around the neglected burial ground on the north side of St Mary's was removed and the area cleared of rubbish, levelled and laid with pebbles. The boundary was marked by stud-stones (since replaced by railings). The Trustees met three-quarters of the cost for this work. In 1751 they paid for the installation of lamps around the library mounted on low obelisks of Portland stone. It was initially agreed that the University would pay for the lighting of the lamps and the oil, but from 1755 this was paid for out of the £100 a year Radcliffe had left for the Library's maintenance. In 1753 the Trustees arranged for the area around the Library to be re-gravelled, and ensured that the windows would be regularly cleaned.

26. J. Green, title-page engraving for Francis Wise,
Nummorum antiquorum scriniis Bodleianis, 1750.

In 1750 Francis Wise published a catalogue of coins in the Bodleian.
On the title-page was an engraving (above) in which the Radcliffe
Library takes its place among the other public buildings of the
University ('public' meant open to all members of the University, not
to everyone). To its left is St Mary's, the University Church. To its right
are the University Schools, where lectures were given, and the Bodleian
Library, where the University's books were housed. Shown to their
right is the Sheldonian Theatre, the ceremonial hall of the University.
Finally there is Clarendon Building, as it is now called, the home of the
University Press. The Radcliffe Library itself was – what, exactly? As
a privately owned and administered Library, standing on its own piece
of ground, it was something of an anomaly. What is more, little if any
thought had been given as to what sort of Library it would be. For years,
therefore, it struggled to find a role within the University, and serve as
something more than 'Radcliffe's Mausoleum'.

Wise had worked hard to become the first Radcliffe Librarian: as a
great seeker of offices, appointments and livings, he had earlier stood,
without success, as a candidate for Bodley's Librarian. Once in post,

however, he was anything but dynamic. His health was not strong, and he preferred to spend much of his time at home in Elsfield, a village a few miles outside Oxford, among his books, his coins and his beloved garden with its miniature ponds, cascades, seats, arches and temples. '[It] will be for some time a fat sine curâ [sinecure]', Rawlinson had predicted when Wise was appointed Librarian, and Wise seemed set on confirming that prediction. He guarded the library jealously, though, and in 1759 had a run-in with no less a person than the Vice-Chancellor, Thomas Randolph. To keep people out of the library Wise had placed a padlock on the door, and in April he received word from a locksmith that the Vice-Chancellor had had it taken off. 'Upon which', he told Lord Guildford, 'I got another smith to put it on again, and told the Vice-Ch's man I would bring an action against which any one who should break it open'. Hearing this the outraged Randolph came and broke the padlock open himself, then sent Wise a strongly worded letter:

> I was informed this morning that you had clapt a Padlock on
> *our* Radcliffe Library. I sent to you to desire you to come to me:
> and you refused to obey. This is to aquaint you, that if you don't
> come, and ask my pardon for this strange, and unprovok'd insult
> on me, and the whole University, I shall cite you into my Court
> next Term.

Ten years earlier the Vice-Chancellor had been ceremoniously presented with the keys to the Library by the senior Radcliffe Trustee. The Radcliffe Librarian was now doing all he could to keep the senior officer of the University out.

In his defence, Wise pointed out that he had received no statutes from the Trustees stating the rules of the Library and the extent of his powers: 'no body yet has any thing to do with the Library, but myself' he told Lord Guildford. For some time it must have felt like a very empty building: empty of visitors, and indeed empty of books.

When Sir Thomas Bodley decided to refound the University Library at the end of the sixteenth century he had taken a close interest in the purchase and gifts of books, and voiced strong opinions on the kinds of titles the Library should have – and not have – on its shelves. There was no such sense of purpose with the Radcliffe Library: from the beginning there had been an uncertainty about the nature of its collections. In 1715 Arthur Charlett had described it as being 'chiefly intended for the Purchase of Foreign Books, Dr Radcliff imagining, the Act of Parliament had already given us [i.e the Bodleian] Title to all printed in England'. In 1749, shortly before the library opened, Rawlinson told Thomas Rawlins that Thomas Carte's *A General History of England* would be the first book placed in the Library, and added that it was 'designed for the most modern books in all faculties and languages, not in the Bodleian Library'. John Pointer, meanwhile, in his *Oxoniensis academia*, published that year, thought the collection would be more specific: 'It is call'd the Physic Library, being to consist of all Sorts of Books belonging to the Science of Physic, as Anatomy, Botany, Surgery and Philosophy. In Time it may be the compleatest Physic Library in the World.'

In 1747 *The Gentleman and Lady's Pocket Companion for Oxford* had reported that "'tis thought in half a Year more the Books will be in'. This proved unduly optimistic. 'I have as yet received no orders about Books for Radcliffe', Wise told Rawlinson two years later. Radcliffe may have left £100 a year in his will for books, but the Trustees controlled that money, not the Librarian, and they showed no inclination to spend it. The first books therefore came through gifts and bequests. In 1749 they received a collection of 50,000 pamphlets from a Mr Bartholomew of University College ('I suppose the Trustees will not accept of such trash' assumed Rawlinson). In 1756 James Gibbs bequeathed to the Library his fine collection of mostly architectural books; this was followed two years later by a collection of law books bequeathed by Charles Viner, and in 1761 by a collection of classical and historical books assembled by Richard Frewin. Two notable purchases were eventually made while Wise was Librarian – the oriental manuscripts of James Fraser (in 1758) and George Sale (in 1760) – but the shelves remained mostly empty and what they did hold was random and without an overall purpose. In 1759 the lawyer William Blackstone, a Fellow of All Souls, suggested that the Radcliffe become a 'Library of a new Species' by housing the Bodleian's great collection of manuscripts. This, he argued, would stamp 'a peculiar and most useful character of its own on that noble structure, which it must ever want if considered only as a supplement to former libraries', but his initiative was unsuccessful.

Francis Wise died in 1767, leaving the Library his fine collection of coins, and was succeeded by Benjamin Kennicott, the Hebrew scholar who had so vividly described the opening of the library eighteen years before. Deeply immersed in his major scholarly enterprise, a collation of manuscripts of the Hebrew Bible, Kennicott spent little time thinking

about the Radclife Library, although in 1770 he did compose a memo-
randum to the Trustees reporting on several matters. The book cases
had been repaired. He had received Wise's collection of coins from his
sister. The upper windows had been resealed and the lead repaired,
'to stop some considerable Leaks'; the upper windows had also been
repainted. The shelves and cases had been labelled and numbered,
and a volume bound in leather, in preparation for a library catalogue.
Thomas Hunt, Laudian Professor of Arabic, had been cataloguing the
Fraser manuscripts for the Trustees. Kennicott's concluding point con-
cerned a matter much closer to his heart, and for the first time one
senses real enthusiasm: he recommended to the Trustees that they purchase 'a very elegant and finely illuminated' manuscript of the entire
Hebrew Bible, by which, 'the honour of the Radcliffe name would be
further celebrated through Europe'. This superb volume, now known
as the Kennicott Bible, had been completed in Corunna, Spain in 1476.
Kennicott clearly convinced his Trustees of its importance, as the following year they bought the manuscript for £52. 10s., thereby making
their greatest single purchase (fig. 27, overleaf).

Kennicott also oversaw, in 1780, the purchase of the Clarendon
State Papers, and on his death three years later he bequeathed to the
Library his own important collection of Hebrew manuscripts. In general, however, the Radcliffe collection had not been much increased
during his tenure, and the Library had languished. Reports of his death
in the newspapers prompted calls for a younger and more energetic
Librarian (or at least a young and energetic Assistant Librarian). No
one was quite sure what the Radcliffe Library contained: one corre-
spondent supposed it was 'one of the first collections in the universe';
another wrote that it was of little value compared to the collections in
the Bodleian and other Oxford libraries, and remarked that 'this benefaction of Dr. Radcliffe has often been considered as a kind of useless
and unnecessary donation.'

Kennicott's successor was Thomas Hornsby. He served as Radcliffe's
Librarian for the next twenty-seven years, and for most of those years
was, in addition, Savillian Professor of Astronomy and Sedleian Professor
of Natural Philosophy. He was also in charge of another Radcliffe
building, the Observatory, constructed on the outskirts of north Oxford
between 1772 and 1794, and also funded and administered by the
Radcliffe Trustees. (A third building in Oxford bearing John Radcliffe's
name, the Radcliffe Infirmary, opened in 1771.) Astronomy was where

27. A page from the Kennicott Bible, 1476.

I. Sir Godfrey Kneller, portrait of John Radcliffe, *c.* 1712.

II. John Smallwell, wooden model of the Radcliffe Library, 1734–5, based on a design by Nicholas Hawksmoor.

III. Part of the model showing the east section of the basement and first floor.

IV. John Michael Williams, portrait of James Gibbs, 1752.
Gibbs holds his dividers over a plan of the Radcliffe Camera.

V. Satire by James Gillray depicting Lord Grenville's installation as Chancellor of Oxford University in 1810. The Radcliffe Library features on the left.

VI. View of the rustic basement, from R. Ackermann's *History of the University of Oxford*, 1814.

VII. The Radcliffe Camera looking north-west from St Mary's church, photograph taken in *c.* 1860.

VIII. The Underground Bookstore under construction, *c.* 1910.

IX. The Radcliffe Camera.

X. The inside of the dome of the Radcliffe Camera.

XI. The statue of John Radcliffe by Michael Rysbrack.

XII. The interior of the Radcliffe Camera today.

Hornsby's real interests lay, and consequently he paid almost no attention to the Radcliffe Library. Only once was he stirred into action. In
1805 Sir Roger Newdigate offered to buy a collection of Romano-Greek
statuary, known as the Arundel or Pomfret Marbles, in order to restore
them and place them in the Radcliffe Library, partly on the upper floor
and partly in the vaulted area below, where people could come and see
them. The Trustees accepted his offer warmly the following year, but
Hornsby protested vigorously, arguing that the statues would deprive
the bookcases of light, and that the visitors would disturb the students.
The bookcases were mostly empty, and there were no students to speak
of, but this did not deter Hornsby from his purpose, for he was, he said,
thinking of the future:

> It may be said indeed that the Radcliffe Library has never yet
> been of regular service to the Student, but does it necessarily
> follow that it will never be opened as a Library? The time may
> come, and sooner perhaps than is generally expected, when the
> original purpose of the Benefaction will be fully and advanta-
> geously answered. Shall we then suffer a Proposal to take place,
> which tends to an absolute alienation of the purposes of our illus-
> trious Benefactor?

Hornsby won his case: the offer of the Arundel Marbles was for-
mally declined by the University in 1808. He died two years later.
His achievements as an astronomer were considerable, but he left the
Radcliffe Library badly in need of attention: its purpose needed to be
defined, and energy and expertise was required to give its collections
scope and coherence. A possible solution came from an unlikely source.
In his *View of the Agriculture of Oxfordshire* Arthur Young, Secretary to the
Board of Agriculture, addressed the problem of the Radcliffe Library.
He approached it as an agricultural reformer. There was, he wrote, little
point in making the Radcliffe a general library, for Oxford was well
enough provided with those; but there was a real need for a library
that specialized in natural history, botany, chemistry, mineralogy, agriculture and rural mechanics. A Professorship in Agriculture and Rural
Economy would soon be established, and the new professor 'would
make a sorry figure without some such establishment'. Young reckoned
that the Radcliffe Trustees had plenty of money at their disposal to buy
a large number of such books: he adduced the recent building of the

Radcliffe Observatory and pointed out that little of the money left by Radcliffe for the annual buying of books had been spent. The matter of the Arundel Marbles demonstrated that there was a temptation to turn the Library into no more than a beautiful exhibition space, and then, warned Young, 'Utility would fly before the schemes of elegance; and plans of Agriculture fade away amidst the visions of *Virtu.*'

Thomas Hornsby was succeeded as librarian in 1810 by George Williams, the Regius and Sherardian Professor of Botany and a practicing physician. For the next twenty-four years Williams focussed the Library's collecting in the manner proposed by Arthur Young. He set about rectifying the 'chasms' in the collection, disposed of duplicates and updated the medical collection with current journals. This required a considerable outlay of money, and so the Trustees supplemented Radcliffe's £100 a year with additional grants. Williams also made the occasional expensive purchase, notably John James Audubon's majestic *Birds of America.* This was issued in parts: Audubon signed Williams up on his visit to Oxford in 1828, and the Radcliffe Library remained a faithful subscriber to the project up to its eventual conclusion ten years later. In addition, Williams saw that the books in the Library were more rationally arranged on the shelves, and worked towards the first comprehensive catalogue.

The Radcliffe library was at last becoming useful. It also remained one of the architectural glories of Oxford, and received an increasing number of curious visitors from outside the city. On 14 June 1814 it served as the venue for one of the grandest dinners ever held at Oxford, attended by the Prince Regent, the Tsar of Russia, the King of Prussia and other royalty, who entered the Library from All Souls along a red carpet (the seating plan is illustrated opposite, fig. 28). The general public were even admitted to the gallery to watch the festivities, although unfortunately their numbers were greatly underestimated. 'The excessive pressure was highly dangerous', reads a contemporary account. 'Hats, caps, and shoes, were flying in all directions; and many at last extricated themselves with their gowns or coats torn in pieces. Scarcely any female obtained admittance for two hours.' Eventually the military was called and order restored; the public could then concentrate on a sight that was 'truly gratifying'. In the middle of the floor, directly under the dome, was a table containing a dazzling array of gold and silver plate (marked B in the seating plan). Around this sat the most distinguished guests, while five further tables, also loaded with plate,

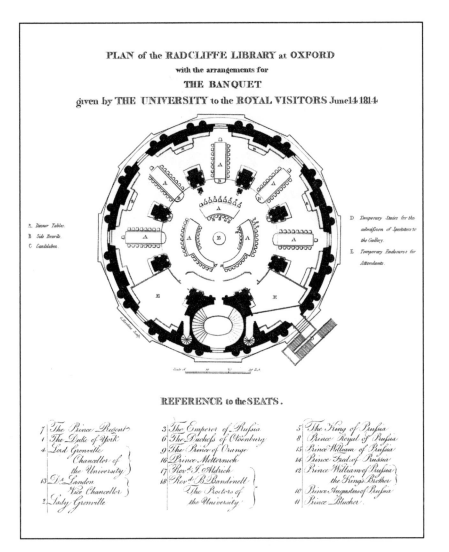

28. G. Hawkins, seating plan for the royal banquet held
on 14 June 1814 in the Radcliffe Library, 1816.

29. H. Le Keux after F. Mackenzie, *Interior of the Radcliffe Library*,
for the Oxford Almanack, 1836.

branched off into the spaces under the great arches of the arcade. In
all, about 200 guests sat down to dinner, the gentlemen in court or regi-
mental dress, over which they wore scarlet academic robes. The room
was lit by brilliant lamps hung from the pilasters, and from a profusion
of silver candlesticks on the tables. The food was prepared at Brasenose
College, and throughout the dinner the Prince Regent was in an unusu-
ally good mood:

> The whole presented a scene scarcely ever equalled, owing to the
> beauty of the building, the perfect convenience for spectators,
> the rank of the guests, and the unique and classical effect which
> the robes gave to the whole scene. The Prince was in high spirits;
> and whenever, on announcing of a favourite toast, the spectators
> loudly testified their approbation, his Royal Highness was pleased
> repeatedly to wave his hand with enthusiastic delight, and to join
> them heartily in the expression of their applause.

At about 11 o'clock the party left to watch a great firework display, 'which
then blazed universally through the streets of Oxford.'

The magnificent interior had lost none of its power, and despite Young's warning about the Library becoming an exhibition space, a number of gifts were accepted which further embellished the room. Two marble candelabra, found in 1769 in Hadrian's Villa and restored by Piranesi, were given by Sir Roger Newdigate. In 1818 two marble busts were installed, and in 1819 six marble sculptures 'of the antique' by a Florentine artist. Further casts were given in 1825, and three years later, 1,000 polished specimens of ancient marbles. Some of these items can be seen in an engraving of the interior made for the 1836 Oxford Almanack, in which the room looks as much like a sculpture gallery as a Library (fig. 29). There are casts of the Apollo Belvedere, the Discobolus, Artemis and the Laocoon. To the left and right of the latter are the huge candelabra, and in the centre of the room, on a round iron and slate table, is a small model of the *Pancratiastae* or wrestlers. Above the Laocoon, a copy of the Warwick Vase stands rather precariously over the gallery balustrade.

After Williams's death in 1834, John Kidd, Regius Professor of Medicine, was appointed Radcliffe Librarian. He continued Williams's work on the catalogue, which was finally published in 1835. Gas heating and lighting were installed, and were no doubt greatly welcomed by readers in the winter months. Kidd was succeeded on his death in 1851 by Henry Wentworth Acland.

Acland was a successful medical doctor and a Reader in Anatomy at Christ Church. In 1857 he would become the Regius Professor of medicine. He lived in a large house on Broad Street opposite the Sheldonian Theatre, numbered John Ruskin among his friends and was an influential Oxford figure. He was also an energetic and successful man of business: he saw opportunities, and he got things done. From 1850 he oversaw a successful campaign to open a University Museum on a site adjoining the University Parks. This brought the various scientific disciplines together under one roof, and created a new space for scientific research and teaching. Acland realized that the new Museum could have a bearing on the future of the Radcliffe Library, and moreover solve an urgent need at the Bodleian Library for an additional reading room. In his November 1856 report to the Radcliffe Trustees he presented a well thought-out and comprehensive plan.

Acland proposed the relocation of the medical and scientific books in the Radcliffe Library, which he estimated at approximately 14–15,000 volumes, to the new University Museum. 'It would be impertinent in me' he wrote, 'to spend words in proving that Scientific Collections are enhanced in value, if their Illustrative Literature is placed beside them instead of at a distance from them; and equally so, were I to point out in detail how the Books themselves are comparatively worthless when they cannot be brought near to the specimens they describe; and how eminently desirable it is that they should be in the Building in which those who require such Books spend their working day.'

Where did that leave the 'splendid Edifice' of the Radcliffe Library, created with such difficulty and care over three decades? The answer, Acland assured his Trustees, was easy, and the purpose noble:

> The Bodleian, overcrowded and greatly expanding, is deficient in a Reading-Room. Dr. Radcliffe placed his Library designedly close to the Bodleian. Certainly this Building could be applied to no more fitting, and no more useful purpose. The literary resources of Oxford would be largely developed, if it became the splendid Apartment for the studies of the treasures of the University Library.

The Trustees accepted Acland's arguments. The University Museum opened in 1860, and the following year the scientific and medical books were moved from the Radcliffe Library to purpose-built first-floor rooms in the Museum. The words 'Radcliffe Library' were painted over the entrance. The non-scientific books (the law books, the Hebrew and theological works, Gibbs' architectural books, miscellaneous literary works, 355 oriental manuscripts) were given to the Bodleian on loan.

Meanwhile a University statute had been passed in 1856 permitting the Bodleian to search for a new reading room not far from the Library ('Camera quaedam haud procul a Bibliotheca'), and on 23 October 1861 the keys to the Radcliffe Library were formally handed over to Bodley's Librarian, H.O. Coxe. The Radcliffe Trustees retained the freehold of the building, but it was effectively now a part of the Bodleian. Henceforth it would be known as the Radcliffe Camera, and on 27 January 1862 it opened as the Bodleian's second reading room. The opening day was rather disappointing, for no one turned up; but the Camera's popularity steadily grew, and it eventually assumed its current role as the main reading room for Oxford's history undergraduates.

Over the next few decades this beautiful but idiosyncratic and impractical building was developed, adapted and extended to serve the

30. The ground floor of the Radcliffe Camera, in use as a book store, *c.* 1940.

needs of a busy university library. To begin with, the Bodleian was des-
perately short of storage space, and the ground floor of the Radcliffe
Camera, still empty and open to the elements, offered an immediate
solution. In 1863 it was converted into an area suitable for housing
books: the arches were filled with glass and the newly enclosed room
was given a floor, heated and fitted with bookcases. This separated the
Library from the surrounding square, but provided another 66,000 feet
of storage space, and the basement was still operating as bookstore until
the completion of the New Bodleian building in 1940 (fig. 30). A new
entrance to the Camera was created in the north wall, reached by an
outer staircase (seen in colour pl. IX).

For the first time, the Library began to receive readers in appreciable
numbers, and space had to be found for them. Additional seating was
therefore installed in the gallery and also on the main floor, which had
already been covered in matting to reduce the noise of the readers'
footsteps. Desks radiated from the centre of the floor like the spokes of a
wheel, in the manner of the famous domed reading room in the British
Museum, and this inevitably changed the character of what had once
been an open and dramatic space.

Functionality jostled with aesthetics in other ways. The Camera's isolated position in the centre of the square was one of its most impressive features, but when Henry Acland proposed that it become an extra reading room for the Bodleian he had assumed that some kind of physical connection would be constructed, protecting precious books and manuscripts on their journeys between the two buildings. It would be simple, he rather blithely said, to create a covered walkway, and he even commissioned Woodward and Deane, the architects of the University Museum, to draw up a design. Their proposal (fig. 31), has an open colonnade on the ground floor, and above it, on the level of the reading room, an enclosed passageway with a double incline for book-trucks on rails. Much to Acland's chagrin, but from today's point of view very fortunately, the Bodleian Librarians did not adopt this solution: '[They] will feel no difficulty in arranging the transit across the street of all volumes that are required by Readers, without a covered way,' Acland told his Trustees, 'and that the additional labour of descending and ascending the flights of stairs which lead into the respective buildings will not be excessive.' Furthermore, he added, 'besides the belief of some that a Library need not have its Reading-Room attached to it, there is in Oxford a conviction that no Architect can unite the Radcliffe and Bodleian buildings with success'. Acland did not accept this, and remained convinced that 'a junction between the two Libraries was mechanically feasible and proper aesthetically'.

Eventually a link between the buildings would be constructed, but in a way which did not compromise the integrity of the free-standing rotunda or constrict movement around the square. In 1909–12 a book-store and connecting passageway were constructed underneath the two buildings (fig. 32 and colour pl. VIII). The upper story of the bookstore employed rolling bookcases of a design apparently suggested by William Ewart Gladstone, who served as a Radcliffe Trustee from 1855 to 1888.

A reminder of the Radcliffe Camera's architectural beginnings came in 1913, when Viscount Dillon presented the Bodleian with the scale model made in 1734–5. It had once been kept at Ditchley Park, the stately home Gibbs had designed for the 2nd Earl of Litchfield. The 3rd Earl had been a Trustee from 1755 to 1772, when the model was recorded as being on display in the hallway at Ditchley. It had subsequently been used as a doll's house and rather roughly treated, and sections of it were now missing. It was partly restored in the 1990s (colour pls II & III).

31. Proposed colonnade, designed by Woodward and Deane,
between the Bodleian and Radcliffe Libraries, *c.* 1855.

32. Section view of the Underground Bookstore
and connecting passage to the Bodleian, 1911.

In 1927 the freehold of the Radcliffe Camera was transferred from the Radcliffe Trust to the University. Since then there have been further changes. In 1936 the railings that had been erected around the building in 1827 were removed; they were reinstalled in 1993. In the 1940s, once it had been cleared of thousands of books, the basement was turned into an additional reading space. More recently, the tunnel between the Camera and the Bodleian was opened to readers and the Underground Bookstore converted into an open-stack library space: the 'Gladstone Link' opened on 5 July 2011. The Camera itself now houses the History Faculty Library, and a more accessible, ramped entrance has been created in the south wall.

Essentially, however, the Radcliffe Camera has hardly changed since it was opened with great ceremony in 1749. Early commentators had questioned the philanthropic motives of its founder and dismissed it as 'Radcliffe's mausoleum'. It had indeed struggled to find a role in the academic life of the University, but it is now an integral part of its library service. What is more, it is one of the finest and most celebrated buildings in Oxford, as fundamental a part of a city's image as the Houses of Parliament in London or the Eiffel Tower in Paris. Whatever Dr Radcliffe intended when he left money 'for the building of a library in Oxford', he would, surely, have delighted in the result.

Appendix

Plates from *Bibliotheca Radcliviana*

The following illustrations and accompanying explanations are taken from James Gibbs' *Bibliotheca Radcliviana: or a short description of the Radcliffe Library at Oxford*, published in 1749. The original plates measure approximately 350 by 200 mm.

PLATE VIII

This is one of the Iron Gates, which are placed in each of the Rustick Arches of the Stone Porch under the Library, to enclose and preserve that Place from being a lurking Place for Rogues in the Night-time, or any other ill Use. Three of the seven Gates may be opened occasionally as wanted, *viz.* that towards St. *Mary's Church*, that towards *All-Souls*, and that towards *Brasen Nose Colleges*; but are to be locked up always before Night comes on, both Summer and Winter.

PLATE IX

This is a Geometrical Section of the Building, through the Middle of the Plan, from the Bottom to the Top, to shew the Disposition of its Inside, the Arches which support the Cupola, the Cupola with its Ornaments, the Framing of the Wood Work, the Thickness of the Floors and Walls. But as this is too small to shew the particular Parts, I have drawn some of them on a larger Scale, to express them better.

PLATE X

A Section, on a larger Scale, through the Middle of the Rustick Basement, a-cross the great Stair Case, shewing the Rising and Winding of the great Stairs; as likewise the Arches, Galleries, Part of the Drum of the Cupola, Cove over the great Stair Case, and Timber Framing, the Profile of the Windows, and the Thickness of the Wall, &c.

PLATE XII

This is the Niche, with its Ornaments, over the *Ionick* Door Case within the Library as you enter it, where the Doctor's Figure stands in his Academical Habit, curiously done in Marble by Mr. *Martin Rysebrack*, a noted Sculptor. This Niche is contained within one of the great Arches which supports the Cupola, over which there is a Marble Table with this inscription: JOHANNES RADCLIFFE MD. HUIUS BIBLIOTHECÆ *Fundator*.

PLATE XIV

A perspective View through three of the Arches which support the Dome, to shew more distinctly the Book Presses, and the reading Desks, in the Library below and Gallery over it. The Point of Sight is taken at a Man's Height, from the opposite Side of the Gallery.

PLATE XV

This shews the Form of the Iron Rail of the great Stairs, with a Plan of it on a larger Scale, the Diameter of it being Eighteen Feet by Twenty one Feet. This Fence is very neatly performed, all its Ornaments, as Roses, Foliage, and the Bases of the upright Bars, are of Copper embossed, and the Whole is capped with a handsome Hand Rail of Mahogony Wood neatly polished.

PLATE XVI

Here is shewn one Quarter Part of each Pavement in the Building; the lowest belongs to the Stone Porch under the Library, which is of a hard Sort of Stone, all laid in Courses, drawn from the Center of the Room, as here expressed. That above, on the same Plate, is the Pavement of the middle Part of the Library, which is of *Portland* Stone, intermixed with red *Swedish* or *Bremen* Stone, drawn from several Centers. This Floor was first proposed to be of black and white Marble polished, but was rejected, being thought improper for the Place, because the Air condensing upon it, occasioned by its Hardness (which commonly, though improperly is called sweating) makes the Place damp, especially where no Fire is kept, and is fitter for Churches, Portico's, Common Halls, and Passages, than a Library.

PLATE XVIII

This shews the great Modilion Cornish, with its Frize fully enriched, which goes round the Inside of the Building, over the great Arches that support the Cupola; I have likewise drawn here a Part of three of the Arches, to shew the Ornaments which are put in the Spandrels, between the Architraves of the Arches.

PLATE XIX

This is one eighth Part of the Ornaments of the Dome in the Inside of it, with their Profiles, letter'd and figured, the Whole curiously done in Fret Work, by Signior *Artari*, an excellent Artist. A, one eighth Part of the Ornament extended on a straight Line; B, the Profile or Section of the Pannels. c, c, the Geometrical Profile from the Middle of the Rose to the outside Border.

PLATE XX

A. Plan of the Frame, or Half of the Outline, or Circumference of the Cupola, shewing the Thickness of the Walls, and how the Dome is framed and supported; a, a, the bearing Pieces for the Truss, on which the Lanthorn is framed, b, b, the Beam or Girder of the Truss; c, c, the upright Posts which form the Lanthorn. The four Divisions in the Plan shew the Timbers which fill up the Spaces within the trussed Frame 1, 1, two half Trusses; 2, 2, the Purloins or cross Timbers; 3, 3, the Furring for the Outline of the Dome; 4, 4, the Bridging on which the Boards are fixed for the Lead Covering.

B, shews the Upright of the principal Wooden Truss, which forms the Inside of the Dome and Outline of the Cupola and Lanthorn and its Framing, all of Heart of Oak, being an excellent Piece of Carpentry well considered, and executed in the best Manner, the Ends of the Timbers being fixed in Shoes of Metal, to preserve them from any Damp that might affect them from the Stone; the Timbers here lettered refer you to the Plan below it.

PLATE XXI

Here are the Ornaments of the several Orders, made use of in this Building. A, is the Base, Architrave, Frize, and Cornish of the *Corinthian* Order on the Outside of the Building. B, the *Ionick* Pedestal, Base, Architrave, Frize, and Cornish, of the Inside of the Building. C, the Profile of the trussed Cornish which crowns the Arches. D, the Profile of the Cornish, on the Outside of the Drum of the Cupola. E, the Profile of the Cornish on the Inside of the Drum. F, the Architrave Moulding of the Arches.

N.B. All the Mouldings, both without and within the Building, are carved proper to their Order.

One of the Iron Gates, which encloses the Stone Porch.

1 2 3 4 5 6 7 8 9 10   20

Jacobo Gibbs Architect   P. Fourdrinier Sculp

A Section Shewing the Inside of the Library

Iacobo Gibbs Architecto

P. Fourdrinier Sculp.

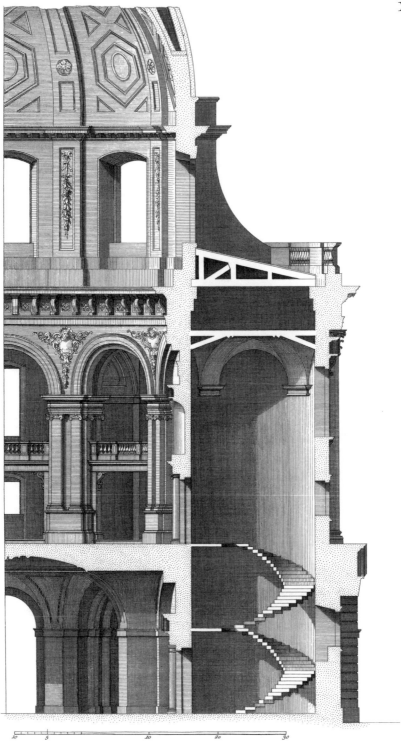

A Section through a part of the Library, and great Stair Case.

Jacobo Gibbs Architecto   P.Fourdrinier Sculp.

XII

IOHANNES RADCLIFFE M.D.
HUJUS BIBLIOTHECÆ
Fundator.

The Niche over the Door in the inside of the Library, with the Doctors Figure.

| | | | | | | | | | | | | | | |
|1|2|3|4|5|6|7|8|9|10|11|12|13|14|15|

Iacobo Gibbs Architects   *P. Fourdrinier Sculp.*

A Perspective View of the Inside of the Library, through three of the great Arches, Shewing the *Bookcases* and *Desks*.

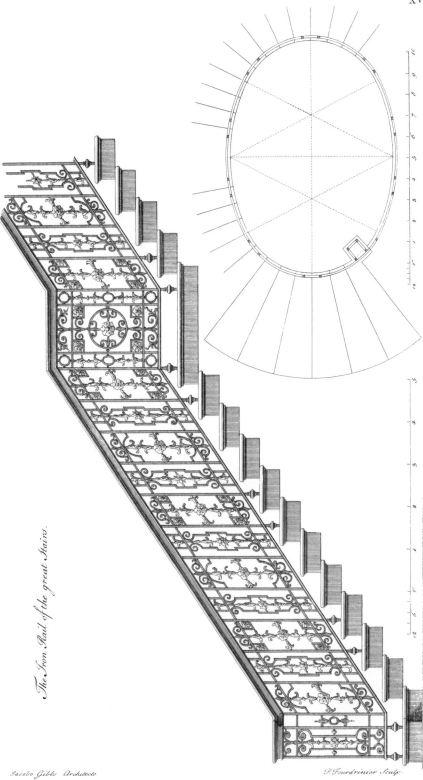

The Iron Rail of the great Stairs.

Jacobo Gibbs Architecto

P. Fourdrinier Sculp.

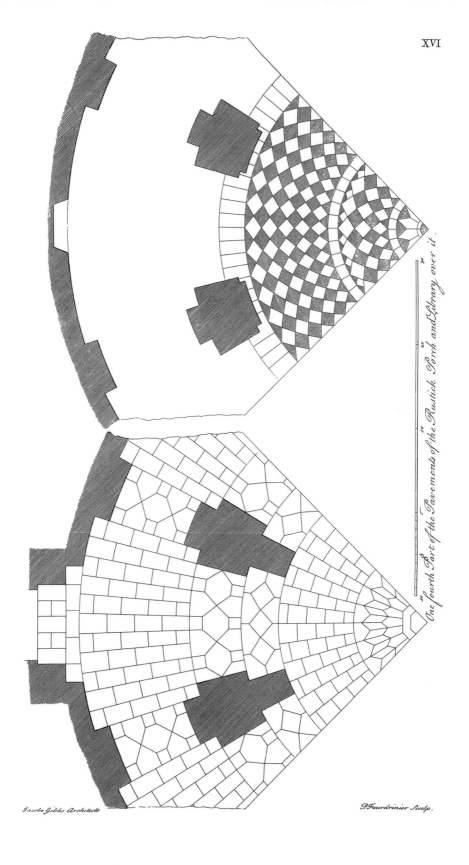

XVI

One Fourth Part of the Pavements of the Rustick Porch and Library over it.

Jacobo Gibbs Architect.

P. Fourdrinier Sculp.

The great Modilion Cornice over the
Arches in the inside of the Library

Jacobo Gibbs Architecto

P. Fourdrinier Sculp.

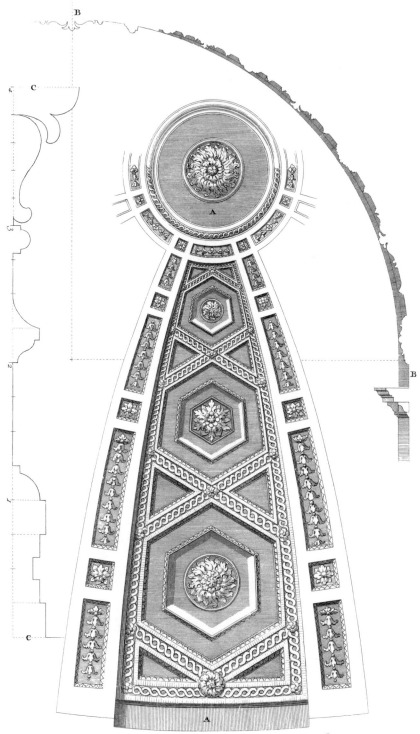

One Eight Part of the Ornaments in the Inside of the Dome.

Jacobo Gibbs Architecto

P. Fourdrinier Sculp.

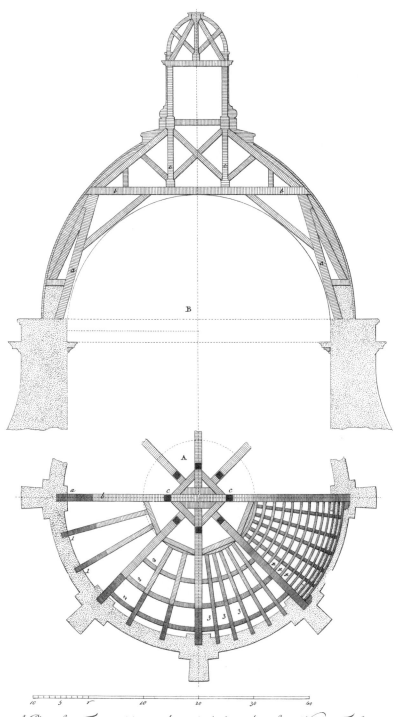

A Plan of the Frame of the Cupola, with the Upright of it's Wooden Truss.

Jacobo Gibbs Architecto

P. Fourdrinier Sculp

The Profiles of the Ornaments of the several Orders used in the Building.

Jacobo Gibbs Architect.

P. Fourdrinier Sculp.

References

All manuscript references are to Bodleian items unless
otherwise stated. Some of the spelling and punctuation
in the quotations has been modernized.

Page 11   For a copy of the notice from the Vice Chancellor see MS. Top.
Oxon. b. 43, fol. 3r

13   'He had little or no Learning ...': diary entry, 4 Nov 1714;
MS. Hearne's Diaries 51, p. 183

13   'every patient who was in despair ...': C.R. Hone, *The Life of
Dr. John Radcliffe*, Faber and Faber, London, 1950, p. 128

14   'Why truly, I would not have ...': William Pittis, *Some Memoirs of the
Life of John Radcliffe*, E. Curll, London, 1715, p. 48

14   'By God! Her Highness's distemper ...': ibid., p. 38

16   'today the Mob as well as Quality ...': Sir G. Beaumont to
J. Radcliffe, 2 Aug 1714; MS. D.D. Radcliffe c. 11

16   '[I] can plead nothing in excuse ...': Pittis, 2nd ed., 1715, p. 97

17   For the text of Radcliffe's will see Ivor Guest, *Dr. John Radcliffe and his
Trust*, The Radcliffe Trust, London, 1991, app. B

17   'the Place of his Education' ...': Pittis, pp. 36–7

19   'Sir, this is Doctor Radcliffe's library': Pittis, p. 6

19   'The Dr [was] but a loose sort of a man ...': diary entry, 1 Dec 1714;
MS. Hearne's Diaries 53, p. 4

19   'I doubt not but there will be ...': T. Hearne to G. Hickes, 22 May
1715; MS. Rawl. Letters 28–29, fol. 130v

21   'great desolate room': G.W. Wheeler (ed.), *Letters of Sir Thomas Bodley
to Thomas James*, Clarendon Press, Oxford, 1926, pp. xi–xii

23   'ruinous little rooms': ibid., p. 22

24   'I am very glad Dr Radcliffe ...': Weymouth to A. Charlett, 8 Jan
1713; MS. Ballard 10, fol. 86r

24   'Doctor Radcliffe's noble design ...': F. Atterbury to Bp. of
Winchester, 30 Dec 1712; R.F. Williams (ed.), *Memoirs and
Correspondence of Francis Atterbury*, W.H. Allen, London, 1869,
vol. 1, p. 174

31   'certain houses ...': Anthony Geraghty, *The Sheldonian Theatre*, Yale
University Press, New Haven and London, p. 22

31   'a fair and capacious Room ...': ibid.

36   'of opinion that since the Doctor's estate ...': Minutes, 27 July 1720;
MS. D.D. Radcliffe c. 48

Page 36 'which by them shall be judged': 7 George I, cap. 13

36 'for fear of a chimneys setting fire ...': Minutes, 10 February 1733; MS. D.D. Radcliffe c. 50.

39 'desirous to compleat ...': Minutes, 23 March 1734; MS. D.D. Radcliffe c. 50

40 'From Oxford I hear the model ...': W. Busby to R. Rawlinson, 29 Jan 1737; MS. Rawl. Letters 28–29, fol. 280r

41 'great improvements': Minutes, 1 April 1737; MS. D.D. Radcliffe c. 50.

43 'able and skillfull artists ...': Gibbs' letter is quoted in full in Guest, 1991, pp. 141–2

46 'directing and supervising the Building ...': MS. Autogr. c. 9, fol. 107

46 'by the pictures I thought ...': W. Brome to R. Rawlinson, 21 Aug 1738; MS. Rawl. Letters 30–31, fol. 371r

46 'not to go on with any part ...' (and subsequent quotes): Minutes Feb–Apr 1741; MS. D.D. Radcliffe c. 50

47 'Masons Work done ...': 'Workman's Contracts and Bills for building the Radcliffe Library'; MS. DD. Radcliffe c. 39, fol. 21r

47 'no small thought is required ...': Guest, p. 142

47 'for the Benefitt of Mary Hearn ...' Trustees' account book; MS. D.D. Radcliffe c. 56

48 'As to Radcliffe's Library ...': T. Hunt to R. Rawlinson, 5 Mar 1747; MS. Rawl. Letters 96, fol. 264v

48 'Unanimity, Integrity, and Candor ...': James Gibbs, *Bibliotheca Radcliviana*, printed for the author, London, 1747, p. [4]

49 'to enclose and preserve that Place ...': ibid., p. 9

53 'This shews the Geometrical Upright ...': *Bibliotheca Radcliviana*, pp. 8–9

54 'I am now every minute ...': T. Allen to T. Hearne, 17 June 1713; MS. Rawl. Letters 13, fol. 30

54 'A godson of Dr Radcliffes ...': B. Willis to T. Hearne, MS. Rawl. Letters 12, fol. 381

54 'I heard of Dr. Radcliffe's Design ...': Hearne to Rawlinson, 5 Jan 1714; MS. Rawl. Letters 111, fol. 28

54 'since 'twas very probable ...': diary entry, 13 Sept 1722; MS. Hearne's Diaries 94, p. 237

55 'an affair, having more interest ...': T. Wise to J. Ward, Jun 1737; British Library, Add. MS. 6209, f. 99

55 '£40,000 given for building ...': Minute, 8 Feb 1749; MS. D.D. Radcliffe c. 50

55 'Almost all the Lodging ...': MS. Top. Oxon. b. 43, fols. 21–22

59 'The most magnificent Structure ...': Thomas Salmon, *The Present State of the Universities*, London, 1744, pp. 42–3

Page 61   '[It] will be for some time ...': R. Rawlinson to T. Rawlins, Apr 1749; MS. Ballard 2, fol. 185v

61   'Upon which ...': F. Wise to Lord Guildford, 18 Apr 1759; MS. North d. 7, fol. 163r

61   'I was informed this morning ...': ibid., fol. 163v

61   'no body yet has any thing ...': ibid., fol. 163r.

62   'chiefly intended for the Purchase ...': 17 Jan 1743: MS. Radcl. Trust c. 3 (9)

62   'designed for the most modern books ...': R. Rawlinson to T. Rawlins, Apr 1749; MS Ballard 2, fol. 185v

62   'It is call'd the Physic Library ...': John Pointer, *Oxoniensis Academia*, S. Birt, London, 1749, p. 145

62   ''tis thought in half a Year ...': *The Gentleman and Lady's Pocket Companion for Oxford*, M. Cooper, London, 1747, p. 13

62   'I have as yet received no orders ...': F. Wise to R. Rawlinson, 19 May 1749: MS. Rawl. J. fol. 30, fol. 211r

62   'I suppose the Trustees will not accept ...':R. Rawlinson to H. Owen, 16 Nov 1749; MS. Rawl. C. 989, fol. 124r

62   'Library of a new Species ...': William Blackstone, *The Great Charter and Charter of the Forest*, Clarendon Press, Oxford, 1759, p. xxxv

63   'to stop some considerable Leaks ...': B. Kennicott to the Radcliffe Trustees, 6 Jun 1770: MS. D.D. Radcl. c. 36

63   'one of the first collections in the universe ...': *The Gentleman's Magazine*, 1783, pt. ii, p. 718

63   'this benefaction of Dr. Radcliffe ...': ibid., p. 744

65   'It may be said indeed ...': T. Hornsby, *The Proposal of Sir Roger Newdigate for Removing the Pomfret Statues*, Oxford, 1806

65   'would make a sorry figure ...': Arthur Young, *View of the Agriculture of Oxfordshire*, Richard Phillips, London, 1809, p. 345

66   'Utility would fly ...': ibid.

66   'The excessive pressure ...': *A Correct Account of the Visit of His Royal Highness the Prince Regent*, Oxford, 1814, pp. 16–18

69   'It would be impertinent ...': Henry Acland, *Report to the Radcliffe Trustees, on the Transfer of the Radcliffe Library to the Oxford University Museum*, Oxford, 1861, pp. 21–2

70   'The Bodleian, overcrowded and ...': ibid., p. 22

72   'will feel no difficulty ...': ibid. p. 14

Further Reading

H. Colvin, *Unbuilt Oxford*, Yale University Press, New Haven and London, 1983

D. Cranston, *John Radcliffe and His Legacy to Oxford*, Words by Design, Bicester, 2013

K. Downes, *Hawksmoor*, Zwemmer, London, 1959

T. Friedman, *James Gibbs*, Yale University Press, New Haven and London, 1984

S.G. Gillam, *The Building Accounts of the Radcliffe Camera*, Clarendon Press, Oxford, 1958

I. Guest, *Dr. John Radcliffe and His Trust*, The Radcliffe Trust, London, 1991

V. Hart, *Nicholas Hawksmoor: Rebuilding Ancient Wonders*, Yale University Press, New Haven and London, 2002

S. Lang, 'By Hawksmoor out of Gibbs', *Architectural Review* 105 (1949), pp. 183–90

G. Tyack, *Oxford: an Architectural Guide*, Oxford University Press, Oxford, 1998

R. White, *Nicholas Hawksmoor and the Replanning of Oxford*, British Architectural Library Drawings Collection/Ashmolean Museum, London and Oxford, 1997

Index of Names